Start Digging!

Start Digging!

Dan Herr

THE THOMAS MORE PRESS
Chicago, Illinois

Portions of this book, in different form, have appeared in *The Critic, U.S. Catholic, Notre Dame Magazine, Saturday Evening Post,* and the book *Stop Pushing!*

ISBN 0-88347-204-X

Contents

For readers seeking the significance of the title:

When Todd Brennan first suggested this book, more or less a sequel to the long out-of-print *Stop Pushing!* (published in earlier, perhaps better times), editor Joel Wells, maliciously referring to my advanced age, smartcracked: "Why not call it *Start Digging!*?"

Foreword

A LITTLE over a quarter of a century ago, Doubleday's John Delaney asked me to write a foreword for Dan Herr's book, *Stop Pushing!* Since Mr. Herr was my boss and Doubleday offered to pay me a hundred dollars (enough money, in those days, for a weekend in New York), I was happy to oblige.

Twenty-six years later Dan Herr is still my boss and he offered me a free trip to Beirut if I refused to write another foreword, so I am still in an obliging mood.

In that first preface I described Dan Herr as a "certified, card-carrying iconoclast," a "Savonarola in Will Roger's clothing." And the *New York Times* review of *Stop Pushing!* began: "With a hatful of well-turned phrases and less-than-gentle paragraphs, Dan Herr proceeds in this book to take the wind out of the sails of almost everything, living or dead."

Has he mellowed with age?

Yes—and no.

Yes, in the sense that this book is nostalgic in its reminiscences of his father, his own boyhood in Ohio, his extended family of wacko relatives, his college days in Manhattan, his military misadventures, his travels abroad, and his long tenure as President (later, Chairman) of the Thomas More Association and publisher of *The Critic,* in the pages of which he wrote the celebrated, widely read, acerbic column from which the earlier book took its title. Yes, in the chapter (so revealing of deep emotional and psychic problems that I was tempted to avert my eyes) he devotes to his involvement with dogs, cats and (ugh!) pigeons.

No, in the sense that even in this retreat to nostalgia he finds little with which to reproach himself. There is no second-guessing here, no "if I had it to do over again I might have considered. . . ." If he was correct in his judgment about something or someone back there in the gloaming, he is still right; if, as he is fond of proclaiming, "I was surrounded by ribbon clerks," they are still back there bungling away. In short, neither hindsight nor history have changed or softened Dan Herr's conviction that being perpetually right makes all the difference.

And the irritating (or the delightful, if one is so disposed to take it) thing is that he was and is just that—right in his opinions, views, insights, even in his apparent snap judgments. And he remains a remarkably acute observer of the "human comedy" of manners, morals and pomposity.

Start Digging! may be a little less vitriolic than was *Stop Pushing!* but more than compensates for that in its wisdom, sharp-edged humor and richly textured reminiscences of an unusual man and his equally unusual life. It's an encounter you won't soon forget.

I would like to add that there is even more here than meets the eye but, because Mr. Herr is as notoriously and vengefully touchy about his somewhat modest stature as was Cyrano about the length of his nose, he is apt to misinterpret such a simile as yet another of what he calls "heightest slurs" and detects everywhere. (We have "brief," never "short," editorial meetings at Thomas More.)

It's true, nonetheless. There's much to savor in these pages.

                                                    Joel Wells

There are things of which I may not speak;
   There are dreams that cannot die;
There are thoughts that make the strong heart weak,
And bring a pallor into the cheek,
   And a mist before the eye.

My Lost Youth
Henry Wadsworth Longfellow

1) One Man's Family

FOR all I know the purveyors of gloom who are predicting the end of the family before the end of the century may be right. Just in case that particular disaster occurs, I would like to record for future historians the exploits and eccentricities of my own dear family in the belief that they deserve a footnote in someone's history of the family as an institution.

My mother's family (who were Alsatian) were reasonable, calm people and, to the best of my knowledge, did little that changed the world. My father, however, came from far different stock—not necessarily better or worse but definitely different. His mother and father departed Ireland during the potato famine, settled on a farm near Venice, Ohio, and brought forth three girls and four boys. (There seems to be a question about how such a German-sounding name became attached to an Irish family. One theory is that an "O" was deliberately dropped along the way; another, that the Herrs were victims of Ellis Island bureaucrats who are reported to have changed names at will. In any event, Irish Herrs are rare, especially in Ireland.)

When I was younger and my memory was better, I could recall the early exploits of the seven children of Margaret and William Herr. All I can remember now, however, are the tales of their later years—tales whose authenticity I will swear to on St. Patrick's Breastplate.

Anna (my godmother) was the youngest of the Herr girls. When I knew her she was about five feet in height and weighed several hundred pounds. She also had a mustache and more than the suggestion of a beard—kissing her was considered perilously beyond the call of duty by my brothers and me. Before my time Anna had married Joe. The added responsibilities brought on by marriage turned Joe—who had never been too vigorous—sickly and he was forced to give up the pleasure of earning his own living. After a time, even the rigors of daily life proved too much and he quietly passed on. (I seem to recall that he had fallen out of a hayloft when he was young, but I may have him mixed up with Uncle Ed who fell to his death from a tree.) Anna's claim to fame was that she may well have been the only guest of the Little Sisters of the Poor who was thrown out within twelve hours of her welcome. And it was all the result of a slight misunderstanding. She was debating with one of the Sisters about keeping her luggage under her bed and to stress how strongly she felt about the matter she crowned the Sister with an umbrella. What else could one woman do?

Our family visited Aunt Anna (who lived in Castalia, Ohio, the home of the Blue Hole or "bottomless lake") several times a year but we children went as seldom as possible and invented elaborate excuses for staying home. In addition to the beard complication, her domicile was one of the most unkempt houses in the Western Hemisphere—my father frequently threatened to report her to the County Health Department. Her dog was vicious and noisy, and a good part of every visit consisted of her haranguing us for not having come more often. Almost as bad were her semiannual visits to our home. She always arrived without notice, early in the morning. Inevitably, within an hour she had fought with my father or had been offended by some unintentional slight. Thereupon she returned to the railroad station and sat in solitary self-righteousness until the afternoon train. Mother always sent sandwiches and coffee to her at noon which she deigned to accept but not acknowledge. The worst part of the affair was that in our small town (Huron, Ohio, population 1,982) such a public incident was soon known to our friends and our enemies. It was humiliating.

Foremost among the female Herrs was Kit. She was a lady! And never let anyone forget it. Tall, snow-white hair, striking figure, regal bearing, she realized she was something special and expected everyone to act accordingly. Her husband Patrick certainly did. Patrick was not worthy of her, as he would willingly acknowledge, particularly when he had had a few drinks—and this she did not deny. Patrick devoted his life to making Kit comfortable, so possibly it turned out to be a better match than her friends had predicted. (Some of Pat's relatives, however, did not agree that he had been blessed by heaven and just because she publicly enjoyed ill health would refer to her as "that drugstore Patrick married.")

For what seemed to us sufficient evidence at the time, we were convinced that Kit and Pat lived as brother and sister. It was hard to connect sex with anyone so ethereal as Kit and Pat always treated her as if she were the most fragile of beings. Kit contributed to our suspicion by periodically announcing that she "never loved any man" but rather gave all her love to the Lord. Just once do I recall Pat reacting to this putdown. At a family reunion when she piously proclaimed her sentiments on love, he said, "Well, that never stopped you living off me all these years—and a good living it was, too."

Kit devoted much of her adult life and her limited

energies to helping priests, including a particularly pompous pastor who gave her inordinate delight by boarding at her home while his rectory was being refurbished. She was a font of ecclesiastical gossip and without warning—frequently with no pertinence to the subject under discussion—she would come up with infallible pronouncements such as (to my mother, when my brother was ordained), "He's no longer your son; now he belongs to the whole world," or (my favorite clerical quote), "If you rustle one cassock, you rustle all the cassocks from here to Rome." In my brother's opinion, her best maxim was: "There is no sermon so bad that you can't learn from it."

Although the Herr sisters presented a united front to their brothers and to the world, they did not care too much for each other's company. As they grew older, so did their mutual irritation. At family functions they represented three armed camps. I recall that Kit was secretive about her age and when she was questioned would only admit to "sixty plus." One day, however, this coyness was too much for Mary, the oldest, who spoke up, "You're seventy-eight, Kit, and you know it." Kit never talked to her again.

You would never mistake Pat for a Herr—he was too uncomplicated. A kindly, white-haired, portly old man (when I knew him), he tried to hide his kindness beneath a gruff voice and crusty manner. But if only a few of the rumors that circulated among the relatives were true, he had enjoyed a wild youth before settling down with Kit. Among his youthful escapades was an interlude as a cowboy, another as a gold miner and a third as a sideshow barker. After being domesticated by Kit, he became a railroad telegrapher and worked hard to furnish

Kit with the luxuries she was obviously entitled to, including the only Edison phonograph in Oak Harbor, Ohio. Keeping Kit in style necessitated supplementing his income, so he became a salesman on the side for a variety of items, some questionable, some indulging his ribald sense of humor—an aspect of his personality that he kept hidden from his wife. He had the exclusive sales rights to Ohio for what was probably the forerunner of the ballpoint pen but, unfortunately, the bugs had not yet been eliminated, so for a time Pat had to change his traveling habits in order to avoid irate customers.

I never knew my uncle Ed (the one who came to a bad end from a high tree) but his wife Kate was an odd one. She was short, very plump and heavily corseted—a combination which caused my father to describe her as "pigeon-breasted." (I can hear my mother saying, "Will, that is both vulgar and uncharitable.") Aunt Kate's daughter died in her early teens and from then on Aunt Kate never had a dry eye in public. If you were to wish her a Merry Christmas, she would reply, "My Christmas is out at the cemetery," as was her Easter, her 4th of July and her Thanksgiving Day. She resented the fact that her sainted daughter had been taken from her while my father's ruffian children continued to contaminate the earth, and she often managed to indicate how unfair this was. Aunt Kate being Aunt Kate, some of us were inclined to wonder about the accidental nature of Uncle Ed's fall from the tree, but, of course, we were too Christian to say so publicly.

John was the bachelor brother. In those days bachelorhood was an exalted state and not the butt of innuendo as today. With his patent leather shoes, his silk shirts, his spats, his derby and his boutonniere, he was a proper dude. John lived in the Knights of Columbus Hotel in Gary, Indiana, but how he earned his living we never did learn. His "profession" must have paid reasonably well, however, because it enabled him to take three months off every summer to visit his sisters and once he even made a long, mysterious trip to Cuba. Visiting his sisters was not, as you might think, a vacation since he spent a good deal of his time taking care of the problems which had accumulated since his last visit and had proved too much for his brothers-in-law. I did not appreciate Uncle John in those days—not knowing then what a bachelor uncle suffers at the hands of his relatives. Adding to my feeling, or lack of feeling, toward Uncle John was his much-discussed public denunciation of me as "a noisy jumping jack." Among his eccentricities that I now consider perfectly normal was his refusal to stay overnight at the home of a relative. Wise man that he was, he preferred, actually insisted on, the nearest hotel. My most pleasant memory of Uncle John was the bountiful gift box he sent at Christmas. It was the high point of our holiday. At least it was until he became incensed over some innocent remark of mine, repeated to him by one of his sisters, and cut out our Christmas bonanza.

The rest of the family consisted of Daniel (I was his namesake) and William, my father. Since these two had married charming, comparatively normal, wives and had surrounded themselves with children, they could not afford neuroses and, compared to the rest of the tribe, were almost normal. But not common or ordinary, of course. My father, for example, was a mighty feuder. He feuded with people and with institutions, but of all his hates, first place was reserved for banks and bankers.

Among my earliest memories was hearing my father raging against banks, and my mother, as usual, trying to calm him. What with children and illnesses and schools, there was always a mortgage on our home. From time to time, when things were really tough, my father had to humble himself and beg an extension of his loan. He always got it, but not without an argument. After the banker deigned to grant the supplication, my father, despite his feelings, tried to sham a little gratitude. But when the banker, following the age-old custom of bankers, proceeded to add a few pious words on the necessity for economizing and budgeting, my father, forgetting his beggar role and his promise to my mother, would fumigate the sacred premises with his righteous indignation. Sooner or later he always made the point that they were doing him no favor—the longer the mortgage the more interest they were earning. My father lived for the day when he could triumphantly make the final payment. He found much pleasure in rehearsing, over and over again, the speech he would make on this grand and glorious occasion. And a masterpiece of oratory it would have been. I am sorry to say that although he lived to be more than eighty, he never realized this, his greatest ambition.

2) Another Man's Family

I WAS born February 11, 1917, on the eve of World War I, and was baptized "Robert." It seems that my father wanted me named after his favorite brother, Daniel, but for some reason my mother declared that name anathema. However, as so often happens, she soon developed guilt feelings and when our old German pastor assured her that one baptismal name was as good as another, I became Daniel. Which may, or may not, explain a lot.

Until I reached the age of reason, I resided in Huron, Ohio, a small town on Lake Erie, midway between Toledo and Cleveland. The weather, like Chicago's, is miserable—hot summers and bitter winters—but in those days we did not know it could be otherwise. There were no Blacks and only one Jewish family. Our minorities consisted of Italians and Hungarians who worked on the ore docks and lived, as the saying went, "across the river." The Episcopal and the Presbyterian were the churches of what was considered our upper class. Because a majority of Catholics were from "across the river," we were at the bottom of the religious social scale. A disgrace we shared with the Lutherans who had fallen from favor when their pastor, after a row with the congregation, bought a house near the church, started a garage and placed a large sign in his yard facing the church: "You Ding 'Em, We Fix 'Em." There was no Catholic school and the public school was considered Protestant domain but I doubt that you could make a case for religious persecution when my sister Florence was sent home from school one day for protesting the recitation of the "Protestant" Our Father—she sat down and banged her desk when the class reached "For thine is the kingdom and the power and the glory."

My mother and father first met in an argument over religion. She was a telephone operator, he was the new railroad agent; she inadvertently gave him a wrong number, he, true to form, blew up; she, according to family tradition, which may well be apocryphal, called him "a fish eater." When he visited the telephone exchange to lodge a complaint, they fell in love. After a suitable period of courting, during which my mother overcame her objections and eventually joined the Catholic Church, they were married. Her first attendance at Mass tells something about the Church in that day. When the time came for the sermon, the pastor sent the altar boy to the sacristy and he returned with eighteen large china plates. Holding them in one arm, the pastor began a harrangue about women who insist on busybodying around the town instead of staying home and taking care of their families. It seems the Altar Society had borrowed his china for a luncheon and some of the plates had been returned in less than perfect condition. As he warmed to his subject, he emphasized his wrath by sailing plate after plate into the sacristy until all had crashed into pieces.

My childhood memories are few. I came along much later than my sister and two brothers ("scrapings of the pot," as my sister Florence has sometimes referred to me when not amused by my actions), and my life was that of an only child since my siblings had left home. My most vivid childhood memory is the shock of being slugged by our pastor—not the china-smasher but another man who collected neuroses as if they were of great value—in full view of the congregation. In those days the altar boys had the custom of returning to the sanctuary, if they had received communion, and spending time in "thanksgiving." Which I did. But when I started to leave the pastor snarled: "Go on back there. That isn't long enough." With all the dignity of an outraged nine-year-old, I replied: "Father, I consider myself the best judge of that!" And he hit me. He was also the pastor who publicly denounced a member of the congregation as a "penny pincher," although I cannot remember the details of that incident.

My sister maintains that I was the most spoiled of the Herr quartet. If true, it was through no fault of hers, I might add, since one of my earliest sufferings came from being forced to stand over the hot-air register until my pants dried—her unsympathetic reaction while baby-sitting to a small accident on my part, an accident all too characteristic of children at that age. She still insists that "the boys" were lazy; for some reason, she could not understand that we were not to be expected to help with the housework which, of course, was women's work. If we left our clothes or other belongings in our bedrooms or in the bathroom she would maliciously hide them in the attic and she actually seemed to enjoy our howls and tears when whatever we needed was not to be found where we had dropped it.

My brother Edward, six years older than I, was the family go-getter. He once even organized his own birthday party, but neglected to tell our mother. She was understandably shocked when the guests began to arrive. In his early teens he had a large paper route; he managed a laundry and dry-cleaning service; he helped run the local movie house; and during one summer he published a weekly newspaper. Unfortunately, I was shanghaied into helping with most of these enterprises—not always to everyone's satisfaction. When he passed the paper route on to me I subcontracted it to four other boys but eventually I decided there was too little money left after paying them off to justify my trouble.

The laundry business also proved a problem. The wife of the town's leading lawyer was a snob—at least I labeled her as such when she insisted that I deliver her laundry to the back door. As did other snobs in the neighborhood at her suggestion. Even then I was a man of the people and refused to honor such a ridiculous request. To save his customers, my brother was forced to take over deliveries in the better areas of the town. When the movie "Three Musketeers" was playing at the Huron Theatre, my brother ran a press release in his paper touting both the novel and the movie, thereby rousing the ire of the pastor who thundered that Dumas' classic was on the Catholic Index of Forbidden Books. The "retraction" which, under pressure, was published in the next issue brought my brother his first national publicity—it was reprinted as a boob item in H. L. Mencken's *American Mercury.*

From his earliest days Edward dreamed of becoming a priest. The doting relatives—he was the family favorite and I was the woebegone—sewed tiny vestments for him and built a miniature altar. His specialty was funerals, which he organized and which the neighboring kids and I were bribed to attend. The corpse was usually a dead bird or small animal if available. If not, he would officiate at the obsequies and burial of one of the many dolls my sister treasured and, had she known, would not have wanted to part with. Sometimes his funeral sermons were so sad he would have us in tears. The most tearful ceremony I can remember resulted from my older brother, not one to tolerate this sort of foolishness, passing through the improvised chapel and kicking the coffin, corpse and all, down the stairs.

Although I have suggested earlier that my father was relatively normal—at least compared to his sisters and brothers—I should note that not everyone appreciated his sense of humor. I can still recall the uproar when our buxom, very buxom, "hired girl" wanted to obtain something from the ice-box. Since my father happened to be standing in front of it, she politely inquired: "Mr. Herr, can I get in there?" To which he answered, just as politely: "Well, you can certainly try, Maude, but I doubt if you will make it." Being sensitive about her rather gross body, she immediately quit. My mother, who was foremost among those who did not appreciate his wisecracks, was understandably furious. Nor did my mother find most of his stories credible. Typical was his tale about the wife and child of one of the railroad foremen. The baby was sickly from birth and the mother devoted full attention to her child, forcing the father to do the shopping, the housework, the cooking, the laundry and much more, in addition to working hard on the railroad all the livelong day. When the baby died, my father went to the house to tender his sympathy. He claimed that the mother was rocking back and forth crying, "My little excuse is gone, my little excuse is gone." He also alleged that when visiting another railroad employee a little girl answered the door and explained: "Pa's at the table and ma's half et."

After a miserable beginning, my career in the Huron elementary school was uneventful. The misery came because one of my first-grade classmates was a mentally retarded but physically advanced child who seemed to me at least twelve feet tall. His mother, who was at school almost daily, claimed that he was the only normal child in the class—the rest of us were the problem. I was chosen by the teacher to be the boy's guide and my duties kept me in almost continuous fear. Perhaps that explains why later in the year I waited too long to request permission to leave the room and urinated in full view of the class—a devastating experience that could account for at least some of my neuroses. Other than flunking eighth-grade algebra and learning about sex from the neighborhood gang, that was my life in Huron, Ohio.

3) New York, Here We Come

MY brother began the tradition of attending St. John's High School in Toledo. He had been invited to live with relatives there and, when he left for the seminary, a similar invitation was extended to me. Unfortunately, I did not get along well with the relatives—through no fault of mine, you understand—and eventually moved into a boarding house. To help pay for the additional expense, I worked as a switchboard operator at St. Vincent Hospital, beginning part-time but soon working full-time. This was an exciting and romantic job for a high-school student, particularly since the friendly doctors allowed me to attend operations and autopsies. (I can still remember all too vividly seeing the aftermath of one I did not attend—an autopsy performed in the middle of the night by a drunken surgeon: he gutted the body of intestines and organs and such, decorating the walls with them.) Among my duties from time to time was admitting patients, and I recall the dust-up when (to save time and avoid unnecessary questions) I took an obviously pregnant woman to the obstetrics unit only to learn a few minutes later that she was not pregnant, but fat.

St. John's High School was an excellent school and my Jesuit teachers were probably like Jesuit teachers around the world. There was our Greek teacher, Father Sammon, who would fire chalk at your head if you made an error in translating—his aim was incredibly accurate. There was Father Ryan who may have been the laziest Jesuit I ever knew and because he was lazy, I was able to pass biology—I was sick when the final examination was given and I assumed he would be too lazy to make up another examination; so with the help of my friends .... There was Father Walsh, to whom I owe the habit of writing—he assigned 500 words a day to our English class and usually threw our papers in the wastebasket, but now and then he would grade them and you never knew when that would be. And, most important of all, a young scholastic, John L. McKenzie, who was to become famous as an autodidactic biblical scholar.

My chief problem at St. John's was that I had discovered the joys of reading and made the mistake of talking too much about my extracurricular reading fare. When I launched into a strong defense of the plays of Eugene O'Neill, the principal summoned my parents from Huron to Toledo and warned them that I was in danger of hellfire. My parents might not have taken it all that seriously, except that I fell asleep on the way home and my mother picked up the book I was reading only to discover the title was *The Diary of a Seducer.* My plea that this was a contemporary Scandinavian classic was not accepted.

The business manager of St. Vincent Hospital was a brilliant French-Canadian nun, Sister Farley, who ran the hospital along the lines of a charitable concentration camp but made it a great success. She had a phenomenal memory for faces, figures and facts and could look at an incoming patient and charge, "You were in the emergency room eight years ago and never paid your bill." Sister Farley and I quickly became good friends and when it was announced that St. John's College was closing, she decided that I should go away to another Jesuit college and found a philanthropist to make this possible. The philanthropist in question had a drinking problem and when he went on a drunk, he would call her. She would send an intern for him and keep him in the hospital until he dried out. One time she learned that a business partner was attempting to take over the business in his absence and she had a guardian appointed by a friendly judge until her problem drinker could sober up. I never met the philanthropist and his financial assistance came solely on her recommendation.

Since my recently-ordained brother had been assigned to attend Columbia University, I selected Fordham as my next stop. Convincing the Fordham authorities that I should be enrolled was not easy; my chief argument was that I was there and they finally admitted me. My four good friends at Forham are all dead now: John McGiver was a distinguished actor; Richard Breen won an Oscar for screen writing; David Crombie, who we predicted would end his days teaching philosophy, became a vice-president of TWA; and John Coveney achieved fame as a classical music expert. My years at Fordham were almost entirely devoted to the study of philosophy—all Fordham students were subjected to ten hours of philosophy a week in both junior and senior years. We were drenched in Scholastic philosophy; the "pagan" philosophers, such as Kant, Schopenhauer and Nietzsche were easily demolished by a series of syllogisms. The lack of a history of philosophy, despite all the emphasis on the subject, was a stupidity I have never been able to understand. The president of Fordham during my time was the golden-voiced Robert L. Gannon, whose main contribution to education as far as the students were concerned was robing the seniors in an Oxford-type academic gown which had to be worn to all classes.

But my education came, not from Fordham but from New York City which, to a boy not many years from Huron, Ohio, was a glorious revelation of how exciting life could be. The depression was ending; FDR was in his glory; LaGuardia was New York's greatest mayor; the Labor Movement was in its ascendency; activists were protesting Franco, Mussolini and racial injustice; the Communist Party was at the peak of its strength and reveling in it. But most important to me, the Broadway theatre was flourishing—these were perhaps its greatest years. In their prime were Helen Hayes, John Garfield, Orson Welles, Maurice Evans, Judith Anderson, Tallulah Bankhead, Luther Adler, Paul Robeson, Katherine Cornell, Ethel Barrymore, Burgess Meredith, John Gielgud, the Lunts, Martyn Greene, and so many more. Rogers and Hart were beginning to change the course of the American musical theatre, and Rogers and Hammerstein later accomplished that change with their revolutionary, or so it seemed then, *Oklahoma.* Unlike the present, talented playwrights were plentiful—Eugene O'Neill, Arthur Miller, Maxwell Anderson (though he was overrated and his reputation died with him), Sean O'Casey, William Saroyan, George Bernard Shaw, Tennessee Williams, John Galsworthy, Somerset Maugham, S.N. Behrman, Philip Barry, Clifford Odets, come readily to mind. I was able to see almost every Broadway play until the war, both because second balcony seats could ordinarily be obtained for less than a dollar and because in college I was the play reviewer for the "Fordham Ram." But the theatre was only part of my New York experiences and I can only say if I had to judge between going to college and living in New York, I would have chosen New York with no hesitation.

When I graduated from Fordham, I obtained a job as a "junior reporter," a euphemism for "copy boy," on the *New York Daily News,* thanks to a friendly priest whose politician brother-in-law had clout. The job paid $16.00 a week: just enough to live on—the food at the Automat was as good as it was inexpensive—and to have a nickel left at the end of the week for subway fare to obtain the next paycheck. (As for subways, my hours at the *News* usually required me to take the IRT through Grand Central and Times Square to the upper west side at midnight or later. I was never mugged and never had a thought that such might be a threat.) The *Daily News* was a thriving paper in those days, fast winning its life-and-death struggle for tabloid readers with Hearst's *Daily Mirror,* whose chief attraction was Walter Winchell. The *Daily News's* lame, even embarrassing, answer to Winchell was Danton Walker—after trying to write a profile about him for the "Saturday Evening Post" even I had to admit he was too dull to be written about. The *News's* copy desk had to check Walker's column with care because he seldom read the rest of the paper and would announce as a "scoop" something that had been in the headlines days or weeks before.

Often copyboys would be sent out with photographers to rush plates back to the office—a choice assignment, since if we combined running and subways, we could collect for cabs and supplement our $16.00. The electric excitement of the city room as a big story broke is hard to duplicate—at other times a city room is about as spectacular as a suburbanite's game room. Among my memories of "big stories" are Hitler's invasion of

Poland; the Graf Zeppelin explosion (the *News* secured memorable exclusive pictures); the debut of the debutante-to-end-debutantes, Brenda Frazier; the death of Pius XI; and the tragic farce of John Barrymore and Elaine Barrie's opening night on Broadway. Nor can I ever forget the night a report came in that a man was perilously perched on the top of a Fifth-Avenue hotel threatening to jump. I was assigned to one of our top photographers. It was a grim and horrible evening, although morbidly exciting. What scarred me, however, was not the shameful death of this sick man but the horrendous actions of many of the mob surrounding the hotel. Their conduct reminded me of the worst horror stories about merrymaking during executions in medieval Europe. Even worse than the hilarity were the voices screaming, "Jump! Jump!" as the crowd periodically grew restless and bored awaiting the hoped-for denouement. Although the victim was high up on the ledge of the hotel, such was the intensity and the volume of the shouts that he obviously heard the call to die and, perhaps, his refusal to be rescued was a response to the fiendish taunting.

Toward the end of my days at the *News,* I worked the so-called lobster shift, from midnight on. In the early hours almost everyone left the office except a night city editor, the rewrite man, another copyboy and me. At that time the chief duty for the two copyboys was to spend several hours clipping news-stories (in duplicate) from other newspapers for the day city editor. These stories were marked by the assistant to the managing editor, an old fart whose most distinguishing characteristics were his ill-fitting toupee and obsequious smile. Every midnight he would deliver to us, in a manner that a king might have envied, the papers he had spent hours marking. One night my colleague and I were so busy we didn't have time to cut the papers so we threw them out, fully expecting to be reprimanded or even fired the next day. When we heard nothing further, we similarly disposed of the papers the next night and when no alarm was sounded, surmised (correctly) that the city editor did his own newspaper reading and couldn't be bothered with the clippings we so laboriously cut out. From then on, for the rest of my days at the *News,* the assistant to the Managing Editor spent eight hours nightly reading and marking the other New York newspapers and, as soon as he left, we dumped them. Our transgression was never discovered, but it taught me that a hell of a lot of work may be unnecessary.

Of all the men and women I knew at the *News,* two had a particular influence on me. Assistant City Editor Russ Symontowne, whose formal education had ended with the third grade, was undoubtedly the best-informed and best-read person I have ever known. Day after day, time after time, he was able—and did not hesitate—to show up his college-trained colleagues and hold his own with the so-called technical experts. My other friend of happy memory at the *News* was the superb humorist (beloved of *New Yorker* readers), John McNulty. I always remember his final words to me when I left the *News* for the Army: "The world is so full of sons-of-bitches, those few of us who aren't must stick together."

4) Now It Can Be Told

EVEN I will admit that my World War II Army experience was a bit unusual. To begin with, and through no fault of mine, I missed basic training—the schooling in the fundamentals of Army life and discipline that every enlisted man without exception must undergo. How basic training passed me by is too involved to recount in detail—and it might well give comfort to the enemy—except to say that it resulted from a rare combination of circumstances involving the formation of a new Army unit.

In any event, having skipped basic training—as well as Officer Candidate School later—I spent the rest of my Army hitch, five long years, trying desperately to hide my shocking ignorance of things military. Unfortunately, even my knowledge of basic weapons was treacherously hazy. (I shamefully recall being interviewed by a group of "untried officers," soon after arriving back in the States from New Guinea, a battle-scarred veteran of the Buna Campaign. I was doing a fine job of obfuscating until one of my answers all too plainly indicated that I had not the least idea of the difference between a machine gun and a mortar.)

As I mounted the military ladder—I never achieved stardom, but it is exhilarating to think that had the war lasted longer I might have, since ours is a democratic Army—the situation became more and more fraught with danger. Obviously a Major, which I had become by this time, could not request time off for basic training and perforce I became adept at avoiding traps that might reveal me for the civilian that I was. Of course, my pride was hurt and to this day I carry a scarred psyche because the General I was aide to (about whom, more later) forbade me carrying ammunition in my pistol (or was it a revolver?). Said he, "I am willing to die for my country, but I'll be damned if I am going to be accidentally shot by a bumbling aide."

Unique as was my lack of basic military training, it was also somehow typical of the Army. Everyone has heard the cliche about the military: There are two ways of doing things—the right way and the Army way. You don't really believe that, however, until you have become a cog in the military machine. When our division, the 32nd infantry, was training in Australia preparing for combat in New Guinea, we were carefully screened for the lame and the halt, for anyone who might be a liability in jungle warfare. These screen-outs, supposedly unfit for battle, were rumored to be returning to the States. Instead, we discovered later, they preceded the rest of us to New Guinea and into battle by several months. Similarly, when we were in Panama, the General utilized the Panamanian jungles to train Puerto Rican troops for jungle warfare based on his South Pacific experience. The training program was judged a spectacular success. But we weren't too surprised when these jungle-trained troops were promptly shipped to the European theatre of war.

When we, the General and I, that is, arrived in Panama, the war threat to the Canal had passed. Possibly our most important duties, it soon became apparent, involved entertaining and being entertained by the diplomatic corps as well as welcoming bully-boy heads of Latin American countries on their way to Washington for more money and guns to help suppress native troublemakers who were supposedly fomenting rebellion. As aide-de-camp to the Commanding General, I assisted in playing host for our own parties and I accompanied him to all diplomatic social functions. This assignment required three special talents: a gracious manner and an agreeable disposition; the ability to down cocktails with the best of them; and fluency in Spanish. In those days I did not drink, my Spanish never progressed beyond *que pasa* and, need I say, being gracious and agreeable was not usually considered among my charms, then as now.

Little Panama had a diplomatic corps that would have done credit to France—it was lousy with diplomats who had nothing to do except entertain each other. And entertain they did—no excuse for a party was too trivial. I may be slightly exaggerating, but it seems to me that the General and I attended a diplomatic function of some kind every evening while we were in Panama. Worst of all, no matter which diplomat or military leader played host, the guest list seldom varied. Night after night I shook the same tired, hot hands, tried to persuade the bartender that I really wanted just plain ginger ale and stood around for two to four hours acting as I thought the State Department would want me to.

Despite my inner anguish, I felt I was doing rather well, considering how poorly equipped I was for the assignment. Disillusionment came soon, however, when the General called me into his office for a chat. Even now I am not sure whether this was his idea or whether I had been declared persona non grata by a unanimous vote of the diplomatic corps. In any event, the General informed me that my "lugubrious face" was doing irreparable harm to our Good Neighbor policy and to the war effort. Worst of all, I was making life miserable for him—and he liked parties.

I could hardly present a convincing defense, even if I had wished to, but I did point out that Army regulations demanded a general officer be accompanied by an aide, or at least I assumed they did. For the good of the service we finally arrived at a compromise.

Each night, in full formal regalia, I accompanied the General to the scheduled festivities, greeted one and all in a manner that would have done credit to Cardinal Richelieu, then quietly retired to our car and went to sleep until the General's chauffeur informed me that the party was breaking up. I quietly returned to the affair, glowingly praised the host and hostess, bade farewells until the next night and accompanied the General home. If any of the partygoers noticed my peculiar behavior, they never referred to it and evidently did not object.

One problem peculiar to Panama was never solved. We went all out to impress the visiting dictators on their way to Washington, assuring ourselves that all the trouble—and there was plenty of that—was worthwhile because somehow it was helping win the war. But it soon became apparent that our efforts were often in vain. No sooner did some of the dictators return to their own countries than they were overthrown or assassinated— the natural consequence, of course, of not staying home and attending to business.

After even a slight exposure to these thugs, we agreed that too many of them deserved the fate they were about to receive, but it was hard to put your heart in your work when you knew the man you were trying to impress would soon be lying cold, stone dead in the palace. Now and then—more often, perhaps, than we realized—a particularly clever one would escape his fate by killing or imprisoning all his real and potential major enemies before he went visiting, but we never did convince ourselves that the war was shortened through any of our efforts.

My life in Panama was not all diplomatic sham. The General did not need or want much aiding (the war had passed Panama by) so, at one time or another I occupied myself with a variety of duties including the Panama Mobile Force Orientation Program. The highlight of this mostly useless activity, dictated by the Pentagon in an attempt to make our soldiers conscious of the "big picture," was a public commendation of my efforts by Eleanor Roosevelt in her "My Day" column. Similarly earthshaking was my only experience with child training. The General's Jamaican housekeeper was the victim of an adolescent son—I am prevented from further description by the laws of libel. We were all reconciled to having him someday end up where he certainly deserved to be, but in the meantime he spelled trouble: whenever he became a problem, roughly twice a week, so intensely tearful was his mother's reaction that she was unable to clean or cook for at least twenty-four hours. General Harding gave me a direct and solemn order to reform the boy—or take over the mother's duties. I will spare you the detail of my campaign and my ultimate disgrace; just let it be said for the record that I failed.

One of the least edifying aspects of my Army job was that it required me to spend a good deal of time in the presence of the Army hierarchy—in the South Pacific, in Panama and in Puerto Rico. Of course, I met only a small proportion of American general officers, but that was more than I wanted and, with two exceptions, found them shockingly close to the caricatures of generals you see in cartoons and read about in comic novels. I tried to reflect as little as possible on the power these men had because I judged that most of them would have flunked any sort of test designed to reveal character traits to make this a better world. (I was later to decide that hierarchy is hierarchy whether it be ecclesiastical, political, business or Army.)

Although I did not get to know him well, I was mightily impressed by General Joseph ("Vinegar Joe") Stillwell, but most of all I admired Major General Edwin Forest Harding, sometime commander of the 32nd Infantry Division, the Panama Mobile Force and the Caribbean Defense Command, for whom I served more than four years. Not the least of General Harding's achievements was his status as one of the many victims of General Douglas MacArthur's lust for power. Which gave me still another reason for finding the great MacArthur one of the least admirable people I have ever met. I don't want to give the impression that MacArthur and I were old Army buddies—our acquaintanceship was blessedly brief and my most poignant memory of him was his demand, "I want each of you to kill me a Jap." This exhortation was the oratorical highlight of his visit to our division in Australia.

(And, if I may digress a moment: It was during this visit that MacArthur's Australian WAC driver informed us she would be in need of a ladies' room rather soon. Since a division training for combat—in those days, at least—had a fairly short supply of ladies' rooms, this was a crisis demanding the full attention of the division staff. In an amazingly short time, a whole company of military policemen was marched out to surround one of the only kind of toilet facilities available—an exposed slit trench. On orders from their company commander, the soldiers smartly turned their backs and the blushing, slightly hysterical woman was informed that the "ladies' room" was available for her exclusive use.)

The MacArthur legend, from the days of his noble campaign against the Bonus marchers to his final failure to undermine President Harry Truman, has been so well covered that I can add little to it. I do recall, however, that when rumors were floating around that MacArthur was considering running for President, a former colleague of mine on the *New York Daily News*, Jack Turcott, South Pacific war correspondent for the *News*, disappeared for several weeks. We were surprised when he returned to Australia since MacArthur was adamantly opposed to correspondents leaving their assignment and previously had shown his displeasure by not allowing them to reenter *his* theatre of war. Later, after a suitable number of drinks, Turcott confessed to us that he had been on a secret mission for MacArthur, interviewing various conservative leaders in the States to see if MacArthur had a chance of winning the Presidency. The message he brought back was that the American people would consider such a move a dereliction of duty. Subsequently MacArthur pompously and fraudulently announced that never for a moment had he considered deserting his troops even to accept a nomination for the highest office in the land. I suppose that some people believed him.

General Harding, was an anomaly—a high-ranking military leader who was a man of dignity, character, scholarship and compassion. Among the many incidents which proved how atypical he was is this one: When he commanded the Caribbean Defense Command, it was his duty to reprimand personally junior officers whose infractions called for less than a court martial but more than a frown. One such delinquent was a scared second lieutenant who, while on leave, got married without the Army's permission as was required of officers overseas. I ushered him into the office and stood by as the General gravely read the official reprimand, then looked up with a smile and said, "Now, don't you ever do that again."

General Harding was also a poet, a lover of literary classics, particularly Shakespeare and the Bible, a one-time teacher of English literature at West Point and an editor. I will admit that in recent years I have harbored the shameful thought that he might have been more effective and more successful as a military leader had he been more of a bastard. But, for my sake at least, I am glad he wasn't.

5) "Purple Heart"

FOR the most part, of course, Army life is a bore—even the bigmouths grow tired of talking about sex after a time and settle into a state of lethargy. Although combat is certainly no bore, it sometimes seems like an anticlimax after the months of preparation. My time in combat was incredibly brief—Japanese machine gun bullets quickly cut short what I fantasize would have been a spectacular career as a fighting man. My foray into combat and the result is best told by a good friend, the superb writer E.J. Kahn, Jr.—a New Yorker *regular and the author of many books—with whom I spent a good deal of my Army time. With his kind permission, here is a chapter from his* G.I. Jungle *(copyright 1943 by E.J. Kahn, Jr., published by Simon and Schuster):*

WHEN your best friend is wounded in action, you are supposed, according to all the scripts, to be right there and to take immediate avenging steps. When my best Army friend—a soldier named Dan Herr, who is very small and looks as if he would fall apart if you waved a rifle at him—was hit, I was ten miles away. I didn't even hear about it until a few hours afterward, and then only through a garbled field-radio message. A soldier in a combat zone cannot, of course, afford to become too excited about someone's having been killed or wounded. My buddies and I were reconciled, when we got to New Guinea, to the probability that some of us would never leave the place. My particular company was fairly lucky, as a matter of fact. Our combat duties did not require

41

us to take an active part in the front-line fighting, and as a result most of us got by with skins unmarred by anything more deadly than a mosquito. There were exceptions. One of my friends looks all right now, but he has a little scar on his shoulder where there used to be a hole and tiny piece of steel in the middle of what used to be a good lung. Another has been lying on his back on a hospital bed for so long that lately the blisters on his shoulders have been bothering him almost as much as his chest, down the length of which a machine-gun bullet made a rather thorough tour. One man in my company had the misfortune to catch malaria just before the Japanese decided to bomb a hospital where he was sent to, and the bombing was fatally accurate.

This story about Dan Herr has a happy ending, but if anybody had asked me to bet when I first saw him after he was shot that he'd be on his feet six weeks later—as he was—I wouldn't have put up a nickel plugged as many times as he was, which was five. We were both stationed at a native village along the north shore of the island, and early one afternoon he was picked to accompany some officers on a trip up the coast aboard one of four small luggers loaded with ammunition and other supplies. They pulled out around three o'clock and were supposed to reach their destination about four hours later. Just before dark that evening, back at our camp, we heard planes approaching from the east. We counted eighteen. Never having seen more than three or four Japanese planes in the sky at once up to that time, we assumed that these planes were ours, an opinion we hastily revised when they got nearer and we saw that they were Zeros. They didn't pay any attention to us. Maybe they didn't realize that the village below them had a lot of Americans hiding around and under it, or maybe, sensing bigger game ahead, they didn't care. At any rate, they flew straight on, and we felt a lot better. Then we remembered the four little boats, loaded with ammunition, out on the Pacific.

At that stage of the campaign the only means we had of communicating with our forward elements was by radio. Every message had to be coded, and it seemed a long time that afternoon before we got a message off, asking if everything was all right. We couldn't help suspecting that if the Japs had spotted the luggers before they unloaded, everything probably wasn't. A while later we got our answer: "All four ships burning. Several dead." From then on, throughout the night, we received a string of messages. Many of them were garbled, but we gathered that the Zeros had dived down and strafed the luggers with incendiary bullets. One of the few messages that made sense was a terse one: "Herr and some others wounded." It is probably only during a battle, when you expect the worst, that you can experience a great sense of relief at hearing that friend of yours has been wounded.

We didn't find out that night exactly who had been killed, how many had been wounded, or how badly hurt those who had been were. We didn't sleep much; everybody sat around in the dark speculating and hoping that things weren't as bad as our imaginations pictured. The next day we got our first real information from an old Australian seaman who had been on one of the boats, had swum ashore, and had walked down the trail from the scene of the attack. In a way, he was maddening. He had been there, all right, and had seen everything that went on, but, never having been introduced to any of the American soldiers and having no idea what any of them were named, he couldn't tell us with assurance which of our men were alive and which were dead. I mentioned Herr to him, but the name meant nothing. When I described him as a small, skinny, blond-haired fellow, however, he remembered him well. "Ah, yes," said the seaman, using the Australian equivalent of *mais oui,* "he got hurt the worst. They machine-gunned him all over the place. I counted five bullet wounds."

It was inconceivable to those of us who had been left behind that anyone of Herr's slight build could be shot that often and survive, especially taking into consideration the probable shortage of medical facilities up where he was. We were sad and we were sore, because it seemed unfair of the Japs to single out as a target a man so patently unable to absorb that amount of punishment. We waited all day for more detailed radio bulletins to come in. We didn't get any—after all, there was a war on and the welfare of a few casualties had a low priority with our signal officers—but at least nobody reported that Herr was dead, and I was grateful for that.

The next afternoon I was ordered to move up the coast myself, in a native canoe, to Oro Bay. Oro Bay is just a small native village tucked under some coconut trees, indistinguishable from a dozen other native villages strung along that thinly populated coastline. I had no idea whether or not I would find Herr on my way up, but I knew that he must be somewhere around there. Before I left camp, I spent some time consulting the other soldiers in our company about what I should take along for him, in case I did run into him. We had most of his clothing and equipment, but we couldn't see much point in delivering any of that to a man who had been shot five times. Finally we decided that the most sensible thing would be a carton of his favorite brand of cigarettes. We didn't know whether or not he could smoke, but everybody agreed that I shouldn't go empty-handed. Even in the jungle, there were certain traditions about visiting patients in a hospital.

I reached Oro Bay just before dark and wandered back off the beach toward some tents I could see at the edge of the jungle. There were only a few of them, scattered around haphazardly; they constituted, I soon discovered, a field hospital. There are various stages of hospitalization through which a soldier wounded in combat passes. When he is hit, if he can't give himself first aid, he gets it from a medical-aid man, who crawls out under the enemy's fire, bandages him as well as he can under the circumstances, and drags him back to an aid station. (Now and then our medical-aid men got shot themselves.) After our casualties had been treated at an aid station, they would be moved to a portable hospital, where a doctor, who in better days would probably have howled at a nurse for giving him a sterilized gown bearing traces of tattletale gray, performed delicate operations stripped to the waist, ankle-deep in mud, in the beam of a flashlight. Behind the portable hospitals were the field hospitals, behind them the station hospitals, and finally there were the general hopsitals, which really looked like hospitals. The establishment at Oro Bay was a field hospital and wasn't very impressive. Herr was there, all right. I found him in a tiny, one-man tent, with screened flaps, marked "Surgery." I could see him through the flaps, but I didn't go in. He was lying on his back on a cot, covered up to the neck with a bedsheet, and he looked dead.

I stood outside the tent for a few minutes, holding the carton of cigarettes and trying to detect some movement within. There wasn't any, so I went off to search for an attendant. I found a medical orderly in the next tent, and when I told him I wanted to talk to Herr, he said my chances weren't too good. "We just gave him a shot of morphine," he said, "and he'll be out cold for hours. And we're evacuating him by boat three hours from now." I asked if there was any likelihood of his waking up. The orderly told me that if he did become conscious at all it would be only because of the pain induced by his being moved. "He's pretty bad, you know," he said. "One bullet fractured his upper right arm, two of them got him in the left arm, and two more got him in each knee. We've got one of the bullets for him as a souvenir." I learned some time afterward that he had been brought there from a portable hospital. Before that, he had received first-aid on a beach, after a dinghy in which he was riding when the Zeros got him was finally rowed ashore. His first treatment had been the standard one given during the campaign. Somebody had come along with a package of sulfanilamide powder and poured it into his wounds. He was conscious the whole while, and at one point he asked a soldier to bring a general to see him. Herr had been carrying an envelope containing a few dollars up to the ground. The soldier, not knowing exactly what was up, rushed to a tent where the general was taking a nap, woke him up, and gasped that a dying man had asked for him. The general jumped up, dressed hastily, ran to the beach, saw Herr, and began solemnly to say the final good-bys he assumed were expected of him. Herr interrupted. "Sir," he said, trying to roll into a respectful position and succeeding only in shedding considerable powder, "I'm sorry, but I guess

I lost all your money." Herr was always a very conscientious soldier.

The medic told me I might as well go away and come back when they moved him. I hadn't eaten anything for some time, so I walked off to look for rations. I eventually found a soldier who had two cans of cold beans. He gave me one, which I ate. Then I went back to Surgery. It was getting dark, and I could barely make out Herr's head through the flaps, but I could see that he still wasn't stirring. The orderly came along and I asked him if Herr could smoke when he woke up. It seemed very important to me, for some reason or other, to get those cigarettes to him. The orderly said that Herr probably wouldn't feel up to smoking for a while but that he'd put the carton on the litter on which Herr was removed, so it would accompany him to the station hospital. "He was pretty lucky," the medic said. "He'll get a nice Purple Heart and a nice, long rest." I didn't feel especially envious.

A couple of hours later four soldiers came up to the tent with a litter to carry Herr down to the beach and load him on a rowboat that would ferry him out to a lugger which served as a hospital ship. They asked me to help them transfer him from his cot to the litter. I slipped my arms gingerly under some of the bandages that enveloped his limbs and the five of us lifted him up slowly. Herr started to moan and moved his head. That was reassuring. It was the first sign of life I'd seen in him. He opened his eyes, and when he saw me he let out a yelp and began talking quickly in a semi-delirious vein. Like most men who are wounded and carried away from their outfits, he hadn't any idea he would run into someone he knew for weeks, and he was startled. I figured that he thought he might be dreaming.

It was about a quarter of a mile down to the loading point, and I went along. All the way he remained conscious, talking in a faint voice and asking me to bend over so that he could hear me. Walking along a New Guinea trail is sometimes difficult when you are alone. It is considerably more difficult for four men carrying a stretcher and a fifth walking beside it. There wasn't any room on the trail for me, so I hopped along through the vines and roots alongside it, trying to stay next to Herr and lean over to talk to him. I asked him how he was feeling, and he said fine, which was obviously a lie, and I told him all the boys were rooting for him and were proud of him, and he asked me how they were, and I said fine. Then I told him about the cigarettes, which the medic had placed behind his head, and he thanked me politely and said they were just what he wanted, but I am not sure he knew what I was talking about. A lot of what we said didn't make much sense, probably, since he was a bit incoherent because of the pain and the morphine and I was mainly trying to keep my balance, stay close to the litter, and promise him that I wasn't going away. He knew I was, though, when they carried him out into the water and rested his litter on the seats of the rowboat. He asked me to ride along, and I said that I couldn't but that I would see him again soon, although actually, since he was going back from the fighting zone and I was going forward, it seemed doubtful then that I would see him for some time to come, if ever. Herr is extremely religious and I am not, and perhaps that's the reason I remember the last words he said to me, as we parted for what turned out to be only a month, more clearly than anything else which happened that day. "I know you don't believe in it much," he said, "but please pray for me." I did.

6) By The Sweat Of My Brow

WHEN World War II was winding down, sometime between VE and VJ days, General Harding was assigned to the Joint Chiefs of Staff in Washington. I hung on to his coattails and came along but, obviously, there was no room in the JCOS for a man with my minimal military talents. However, the General managed to have me assigned to the *Infantry Journal,* one of the several military service magazines, all of which were more or less dedicated to promoting a particular service, as much as security regulations would permit. The *Infantry Journal* had expanded to include all sorts of peripheral activities, particularly distributing paperbacks—a new development in the American book trade—to army units throughout the world. My duties did not change much; I still acted as an aide, this time to Colonel Joseph Greene, a brilliant but somewhat erratic editor. I suspect my biggest accomplishment was to find the cause of innumerable complaints from customers who had ordered books published by *Infantry Journal* but had never received them. To the surprise of everyone, the culprit turned out to be a very efficient manager of the Order Department who was so paranoid about keeping up with her work that at the end of each day she simply tore up and flushed down the toilet the orders that had not been processed. Thus she proudly started each new day with a clean in-basket.

When we needed an editor for our publication, *Armed Forces Digest,* I arranged for my brother-in-law Ben Olds to be transferred from his Army public relations assignment in New York City to the *Journal.* Ben, my sister and I rented a small house in Georgetown and settled down to a happy and peaceful year.

But peace and quiet proved too debilitating and Ben and I decided to leave the *Journal,* return to New York and take our chances with free-lancing. We had published our first article before the war—an indictment of Swing based on our love of Jazz, our weekly visits to Harlem's Apollo Theatre and our friendship with Jelly Roll Morton (who sported a diamond in a front tooth) and Teddy Wilson. It appeared in *Scribner's Commentator,* an odd sort of right-wing magazine that added nothing to the distinguished reputation of the old *Scribner's.* We argued: "Swing could have won for jazz the important place it deserves in American music had it not been for the degrading, killing imprint of the Jitterbug."

I free-lanced with Ben until he tired of the insecure life and took on a steady job with *Family Circle.* For a time I collaborated with David Dempsey, a novelist and literary critic. Finally, I went on my own. I soon discovered that magazine writing, at least at the beginning stage, would not keep me at even a subsistence level, but thanks to my *Infantry Journal* connections, I was able to receive regular assignments from the Army. I wrote a number of "Armed Forces Talks" for the Army Orientation Program, and I still have pangs of conscience when I think of the thousands and thousands of soldiers who were forced to listen to my pompous homilies. I pontificated on such subjects as "What makes an outfit tick?"; "What's the score?"; "Don't be a sucker!"; "Wanted: Leaders." Ben and I were asked to write the Geopolitics section of a Senior ROTC text book. We had no idea what the word meant, but because we needed the money we joyfully accepted the assignment. With the help of every reference book we could find, we wrote learnedly about power and its sources; analyzed and judged the United States and the major countries of the world ("Very big, China. . . ."). (In looking back at our opus after four decades, I was gratified to see that at least we predicted "the struggle for control of oil reserves will continue unabated.")

But this military hack work was simply to keep alive. My main interest was in magazine writing and before eventually deserting free-lancing, I had contributed a number of articles to *The Saturday Evening Post,* as well as to *Family Circle, Coronet, McCalls, Life* and Pageant. I wrote on a variety of subjects and was willing to try almost any assignment. Under an "Anonymous" by-line, I told the heart-rending story of how one war-time marriage failed—"After four years, my wife and I are ready to admit that we can't make a go of it. Our problem was the housing shortage. Because of it we had to move in with my wife's parents who were boors and busybodies." The article ended with this heart-rending plea: "It strikes me that, if the American people could be shown what the housing shortage means in terms of human lives and made to think of the marital wreckage it has caused, they would insist that something be done. And when the people of the United States are determined, it is seldom that anything can stand in their way." Somehow I doubt that this plea did much for the housing crisis.

I also tried my hand at ghost writing, doing a crybaby piece for a Congressional Medal of Honor winner, telling why he re-enlisted in the Marine Corps. Working with him confirmed my suspicion that a lack of education and perhaps even a lack of intelligence helps to make heroes—sometimes they just don't know enough to be scared. My chief problem with this particular Medal-of-Honor winner was that I had difficulty persuading him he could not frame the check we received from the magazine.

The first article Ben and I sold to the *Post* was, "Where's that Nurse?" in which we predicted—accurately, as it turned out—a future shortage of nurses. We followed this with "Beware of Gyp Jewelers," the story of how the Jewelers' Vigilance Committee helps to protect consumers. In *America's Host to Potentates*, I wrote of Stanley Woodward, at that time the State Department's Chief of Protocol, the man in charge of hosting visiting dignitaries. Woodward himself was not much help but I did collect interesting sidelights from his staff. Among these: King George and Queen Elizabeth were preceded by a five-page report recommending heavy blankets, despite Washington's notorious summer heat; plenty of steaks and chops; certain brands of liquor most pleasing to the royal palate; and an exclusively private room for pressing and airing the queen's wardrobe. Madame Chiang Kai-shek sent word ahead that the sheets on her bed must be changed whenever she rested, several times a day if necessary. Visitors from the tiny Indian state of Nepal announced that they would bring their own food and cooks. Crown Prince Saud, of Saudi Arabia, warned that liquor and pork should not be served.

My brother tipped me off that Harry E. Munsey of Fostoria, Ohio, whose Rogers Company produced centennial pageants and other amateur extravaganza throughout the country, was worthy of an article and the *Post* editors agreed. Munsey's genius was in realizing that most towns and small cities in America had a similar history so with very few changes, a basic pageant could be adapted to most historical occasions. His productions commemorated the Battle of Antietam, the birth of Steubenville, Ohio, and the death of Will Rogers. They entertained fraternal orders, women's organizations, churches, schools, volunteer fire departments and luncheon clubs. Munsey's directors ranged from Brooklyn to the remote fastnesses of Upper Ontario, and, on behalf of industrial and agricultural associations, they glorified papermaking, railroading, peach growing, peony culture, and the breeding of longhorn cattle. Designed primarily for entertainment and money raising, Rogers' shows had few cultural pretensions and were written to satisfy as easily as possible the Thespian urge that lurks at some time in the soul of nearly everyone.

But the highlight of my free-lancing career—it resulted in my chief claim to fame, a half-million dollar libel suit—was "The Captain They Couldn't Blow Down" for the *Saturday Evening Post.* This was a profile (written with David Dempsey) of Commodore Harry Manning of the *USS America,* a man we described as "a storm-battered crustacean who holds the somewhat unorthodox conviction that the captain is still master of his ship, come hell, high water or the maritime unions. A man whose principles, when aroused, are happily matched by an uninhibited vocabulary and the zeal of a tent-meeting revivalist, Manning looks upon himself as a modern Captain Ahab, pursuing the evils that have reduced America's transatlantic luxury fleet to its present low state of one ship." It was ironic in view of what happened later that Manning was opposed to the article, cooperated as little as possible, and agreed only because the U.S. Lines put pressure on him. Manning led an

action-packed life, including time spent as a navigator
for Amelia Earhart. He was on her last fatal trip but at
Hawaii was summoned back to sea-duty—she flew on
and was never seen again. Oddly for a seaman, Manning was subject to sea-sickness, continually troubled
whenever the weather turned nasty.

The problem that brought on the libel suit was Harry
Manning's struggle with a small union, the Masters,
Mates and Pilots (AFL). Eventually he triumphed, despite a 28-day strike by the Union. We thought we presented the dispute objectively, but the Union thought
otherwise and the *Post,* Commodore Manning and David
and I were charged with conspiracy. It was alleged spe-
cifically that "on or about February 28, 1948, at the city
of Philadelphia, the defendants, pursuant to the afore-
said plan and conspiracy to defame the plaintiff, con-
triving and wickedly and maliciously intending to injure
the plaintiff, did falsely, wickedly, maliciously, intentionally and willfully compose for delivery for publication, print, publish and widely circulate, and did cause
to be printed, published and widely circulated in and
about the cities and villages of the United States, Canada
and in many principal cities of the world, the false, scan-
dalous and defamatory article . . . of and concerning the
plaintiff, and of its occupation and methods of doing
business, and standards of conduct in carrying on its
business."

Although it seemingly has not gone down in the an-
nals of jurisprudence, that leading legal light, Justice
McNally of the Supreme Court of New York County, in
what we considered a brilliant milestone decision, dis-
missed the Union's complaint, explaining, "Words which
are not libelous in themselves cannot be made so by
innuendo."

I finally decided it was time to give up free-lancing and try to earn an honest living. There were too many problems involved, the most critical being that no matter how successful you became, you could not gauge how long your money would have to last, and you were never comfortably secure. An article that you were working on for weeks could blow up for one reason or another, even though a specific magazine had expressed interest. I realized I did not have the emotional stamina for the free-lance life. I needed a steady job.

I moved to a job, which has lasted almost forty years, and it occupied my full attention for a time. But the lure of seeing my name in print proved to be strong and I resumed free-lancing in my off-hours. With two differences, however: I now had a steady job with a regular income and, with a few exceptions *(New York Times Op-Ed)*, I directed my outpourings to the Catholic press. For years I wrote a column "Stop Pushing" for our own magazine, *The Critic,* and for some months I wrote a column, "With Humble Pride," which was syndicated to a number of diocesan newspapers. Today it would be considered thin gruel but in those days, anyone who spoke somewhat bluntly in the Catholic press became a subject of controversy. The letters to the editor prompted by my column were only exceeded, I think, by those which erupted later during Andrew Greeley's tenure as a Catholic columnist. One paper dropped my column because of protests, only to pick it up again when the other side was heard from.

My profiles for a number of Catholic magazines—many of which are no longer published—ranged from a Chicago cop to Chicago's Cardinal Stritch and from Catholic activist Edward Marciniak to Cardinal John Wright. I also sounded off on a range of topics, most frequently in *U.S. Catholic* (creatively edited by Robert Burns, a genial and helpful friend from my earliest days in Chicago). Whether it's my nature, or whether in my wisdom I decided it was the way to go, I usually succeed in being controversial, even without trying. For example, in a rather calm and reasoned article, "Why Priests Should Wear Roman Collars," this almost parenthetical remark brought bitter reaction:

"One other argument for returning to the Roman collar is the unfortunate but inescapable fact that most priests and ex-priests have about as much clothes sense as an iguana. Whether it is just their nature or possibly the result of seminary training, priests in mufti and ex-priests stand out like neon signs because of their outlandish clothes: a pink seersucker suit, blue walking shorts on beefy thighs parading down a busy city street, hand-painted ties, combinations of shirts and ties and suits that might have given Salvador Dali pause—these are only a few horrifying examples that I can attest to personally." I was surprised and hurt that many priests and so-called ex-priests took exception to my obviously well-meaning words.

7) The Rover Boys Abroad

SOME wiseacre once proclaimed that travel is ninety percent anticipation and ten percent reminiscence. I'm inclined to agree, except that I would increase the percentage for reminiscence. Thanks to the Army, I traveled to Australia, New Guinea, Hawaii, New Caledonia, and touched almost all of the Caribbean Islands. As a civilian, I continued my journeys. For more than thirty years my brother and I traveled extensively every summer, visiting Haiti, California, various parts of Canada, Mexico, New England and, finally, Europe.

Our mother accompanied us on some of our pre-European tours and it was on a trip to Canada that an adventure occurred which might best be called, "The Night We Took Our Mother to a Whorehouse."

The three of us had been in Quebec and decided to return to Montreal a day early, even though we had no hotel reservation. We did not expect a problem since there were many motels between the two cities. However, as we neared Montreal and night was approaching, we began to worry because several motels en route had signs proclaiming "No Vacancy." We passed by the church of Saint Maria Goretti and my brother, who tended to be pious in those days, said, "We'll pray to Saint Maria Goretti—she will find us a room." It was only a few minutes later that we noted a motel with a "Vacancy" sign. And sure enough, one large room with two beds was available. We were somewhat mystified by a card on each bed, "Please remove the bedspread," but we assumed this was a French-Canadian peculiarity. We went out to eat at a nearby restaurant and because it had been a long day, retired early. A few hours later I was awakened by a good deal of noise outside our room. I went to the door and heard the proprietor arguing with potential customers about the prices he charged for girls—there seemed to be a sliding scale depending on several factors, better left unnamed. I realized that we were occupying a room in a brothel and woke my mother with the news. She replied, "They're only having a good time. Go back to sleep." Then I informed my brother of our predicament but he, too, was sleepy and advised waiting until morning. I emphasized, somewhat hysterically, the consequences of leaving a house of prostitution in daylight. They finally begrudgingly agreed; we checked out and, fortunately, found a hotel in Montreal.

After I more or less stopped traveling, I was complaining to one of my colleagues that I would be a lot better off if I had the money I had spent on traveling. He wisecracked: "Ah, but you have your memories." He is right, of course, even though at a time when memories might mean the most, they have tended to slip away. But I do recall life at its luxurious best on our many *SS France* voyages; the glories of Chartres, Mont-Saint-Michel, Matisse's Chapel of the Rosary in Vence, and Le Corbusier's Chapel at Ronchamp; the night in Paris when our hotel was bombed, presumably by Basque partisans; the magnificence of the English theatre (where we saw most of Shakespeare and Shaw and Ibsen and the first plays of Harold Pinter, Tom Stoppard, David Storey, and the theatrical stars of our time—Olivier, Gielgud, Gertrude Lawrence, Maggie Smith, Ingrid Bergman, Paul Scofield, Ralph Richardson, Alec Guinness and dozens more); our private audience with Pope John XXIII, when he smilingly gave me a personal homily on books (the Old Testament tells of a man who swallowed a book—you have a lot of books which you want people to swallow); presenting to Paul VI the Thomas More Medal, not noting that for some reason the medal maker had encased it in white powder—the Pope was not amused); the admission by the Vatican's Monsignor, later Archbishop, Ernesto Cardinale that when Pius XII died, he had come away from the death with Volume I of H.L. Mencken's *American Language* and would be eternally grateful if I could get Volume II for him (which I did); and finally, the memory of a sometime traveling companion who is easily bored and shows his boredom by sleeping and almost immediately snoring, embarrassing us during a homily by Paul VI, during a session of the House of Lords in London, and a during a performance of Othello, starring Laurence Olivier, with the Queen and Prince Philip only a few rows away.

After I decided that my European travel days were over, I made up a list of 66 things every traveler should know before setting forth. Among them:

Husbands and wives should never travel together—they inevitably fight, mostly in hotel lobbies.

Franco's Valley of the Fallen is as depressing and ridiculous as Victor Emmanuel's preposterous monument in Rome.

Don't go looking for people to tip—if they don't find you, too bad for them.

In Rome, visit no more than three churches (to paraphrase an esteemed politician: if you've seen one Roman church, you've seen them all).

In choosing a restaurant, you can have scenery or good food but seldom both.

In choosing a restaurant, you can have entertainment or good food but seldom both.

Belgium is about as exciting as Milwaukee.

On a cruise or a tour, make friends slowly.

All hotel cashiers are disagreeable.

Don't waste money on "church treasuries."

Most people will never acquire a taste for tripe.

It's less painful if you reconcile yourself in advance to being unfairly relieved of at least $100 by unscrupulous merchants, guides, waiters, etc., somewhere on the trip.

The Folies-Bergere would no longer shock even a Colonial Dame.

Whenever possible, avoid German tourists.

My most vibrant memories, however, are our several trips to Ireland. With my usual understatement, I might submit that our first trip was a disaster—not the fault of Ireland but the fault of too many technicolor movies, too many songs of Erin's charms, too many Irish-American tales of the glories of the Auld Sod. Whatever the reason, as I wrote in *The Critic,* Ireland struck me as "a dreary and drab land, burdened with a tragic past and boasting mighty little future." I went on to advise tourists that "Ireland is a mistake. Those who have thrilled to Frace and Italy would do well not to venture far from Shannon Airport. To paraphrase Fred Allen, if the first prize in a contest is one week in Ireland, the second prize should be two weeks in Ireland."

Warming to my subject, I complained of the "spirit of futility and decay that strikes a stranger in the face as soon as he arrives. He sees not the happy, carefree Irish he has heard about, but Irish burdened with cares, struggling with problems that seemingly have no solution. These are a people with more than a hint of servility in their manner—not the proud, pugnacious Irish of legend." At the end of my blast, I tried to dilute the vitriol with a few patronizing words about the faith in Ireland and the charm of the Irish people. I solemnly announced that I would "still be wearing a green tie come next Saint Patrick's Day (though possibly the color may be more subdued than in the past)." However, I couldn't resist one last gibe, a toast: "Here's to the Auld Sod and the quickest way out of it."

I wasn't entirely surprised by the vehement reaction— probably the bitterest and most numerous letters resulting from anything I have written. There were the inevitable blasts from Irish-Americans, but there were also a deluge of letters from Ireland. I had not anticipated that my column would be picked up by Irish newspapers. Among the offended was the humorist John D. Sheridan, who advised me to get my ulcers seen to. From novelist Mary Purcell came this:

> His father's patria, not for him—
> Too medieval, dull and dim!
> He found the food and lodging grim.
> His tastes are sybaritic.
> Thus peeved, this divil of a scribe,
> With many a hurtful jeer and gibe,
> Writes Ireland off in a diatribe
> And prints it in his *Critic.*

My favorite quote came from an interview by an enterprising Irish reporter with the manager of a Dublin hotel I had criticized. Said he, "I remember Mr. Herr well. He was a most disagreeable guest."

Having rid myself of my phony illusions, my subsequent trips to Ireland were all that any traveler could ask for, particularly a glorious ten days on the Shannon River (only in Ireland would a stranger be entrusted with a 38-foot cabin cruiser after a $50 deposit and a 15-minute instruction). I did public penance in subsequent issues of *The Critic* and later wrote at length about my many happy experiences in Ireland. My only qualification was the quality of Irish cooking: pointing out that Irish bacon, eggs, bread and butter are the best to be found anywhere, but that everything else is cooked to the point of tastelessness (as in England) and that vegetables are particularly punished for daring to have any distinguishing features. I can still recall ordering in a Dublin restaurant what was listed as "boiled bacon" and which I was sure, because of an obvious typographical error, was broiled bacon. The error, however, proved to be on my part—I was served boiled bacon with a creamed parsley sauce. It proved to be just as bad as it sounds. (In answer to the question "Where can you find typical Irish cooking in Chicago?", columnist Mike Royko suggested: "Walgreen's.")

My change of heart about Ireland came not only because I had grown in age and grace, but because the high points of my trips were visits with long-time friends, Anne and Brian Friel and their family. Through the years their friendship has been a very cheerful part of my life. (Brian, of course, is the distinguished Irish playwright and short story writer who, I am proud to say, dedicated his memorable drama of the civil war in Ireland—"The Freedom of the City"—to me.)

We had many happy days in Ireland; to reread my original comments about that land makes me admit that all the critics who denounced me at the time were right. I feel a little bit like the smart-ass actor who a few years ago was starring in a movie in Ireland. He was drinking at a country inn with other members of the cast when a little girl from a neighboring table asked for autographs. The other actors and actresses wrote appropriate friendly sentiments. The star scrawled an obscenity. Later, when her father noted the obscenity, he proceded with one blow to break the offender's jaw. The star was flown back to the United States for surgery delaying the movie for eight days.

Fortunately, the only blows aimed at me were verbal.

8) A Job For All Seasons

IN the summer of 1948 I decided that free-lancing was not for me, that a regular paycheck would greatly help my morale which had been suffering of late. For reasons that are obscure to me now, I placed an ad in a magazine distributed primarily to priests and, sensibly enough, called *The Priest.* I received only one answer: ironically, not from a priest but from John C. Tully, president of the Thomas More Library and Bookshop in Chicago. At his invitation I journeyed to Chicago for an interview. That I was offered the job as manager of his bookshop and that I accepted tells how desperate both Tully and I were: he, because several managers had come and gone during preceding years; I, because it was my only opportunity for a much-needed (albeit low-paying) job. Tully had to overlook that we disagreed socially, politically, theologically, and almost every other way two people can differ. On my part, the bookshop, upstairs over a churchgoods emporium, was a shambles; Tully loved to pontificate at length on almost any subject without any encouragement; and the staff, it was evident from a quick glance, was, at best, a collection of oddities.

And so I joined Thomas More (we chose a new name, "Thomas More Association," which seemed in keeping with the myriad activities we were about to embark on). For better or worse, Thomas More and I have been inseparable for 38 years, and counting.

Obviously, no one should attempt to compress 38 years' experience in fewer than twelve volumes. But though humility has never attracted me, I can appreciate that even loyal readers might begin to falter after the first few volumes. Some sort of limitation is necessary. I have therefore resolved to forego dwelling on such mighty themes as "Bastards I have known through the years," an omission which will not only save considerable space but may preserve me from threats of libel. For my own peace of mind I will also spare you a recounting of the inevitable sorrows, crises and disasters that we have been plagued with at Thomas More. Nor will I burden you with details of man's (and woman's) inhumanity to me. (I will not even detail my innermost feelings when proudly picketing Loyola University and the Illinois Club for Catholic Women because a silly rich woman denied black children from Holy Name Cathedral School the use of a swimming pool which her pet organization shared with the University.)

What follows, then, are the stories, personalities and events that I can still remember with some degree of accuracy—in fact, cannot forget, even if I tried. Because Thomas More has moved four times during my pontificate and because I am a notorious throw-it-outer, there now exist almost no historical records to prove or disprove my memories.

Thomas More came into being when a small Catholic book store in Chicago went bankrupt. At the request of a Servite priest who had made the Sorrowful Mother Novena a phenomenally successful devotion, Tully, a retired banker and manufacturer, advanced $10,000 to purchase the "assets" of the bankrupt store. The priest promised that he would furnish volunteers to run the bookshop and to publicize it. Unfortunately for John Tully, a week later the priest was removed from his position and Tully was left with an almost stillborn organization. Finally he decided that if for no other reason than to safeguard his investment, he would have to become active. Having made that decision, he found enjoyment in his new role and worked hard to make the bookstore a vital activity.

Through the years the Association sponsored the widest possible variety of activities—within the bounds of our not-for-profit charter, of course. Among them: the stellar literary magazine, *The Critic;* the Thomas More Book Club; the Center For Religious Art (an idea whose time had gone); numerous newsletters, including *Overview, Markings, Context, Sola, Mysterion, Catholic Thinkers In The Clear, Source* and *Us;* lectures and (in cooperation with Rosary College) symposia which featured almost every distinguished American Catholic writer and speaker, some who were not Catholic, and a few from other countries; the Theology Book Club; the Sisters Book League; the Don Bosco Book Club; *Addenda* (an innovative "cassette magazine") and several hundred individual cassette programs; the Catholic Book Annual; the Thomas More Press and—well, you get the idea.

When I came to Thomas More, John Tully's extremely conservative economic and political convictions had grown rigid. The week before I came he had announced to the staff that because inflation was probably the worst evil facing America, he intended to do something about it: they could expect no raises, now or in the future. Looking back, I decided he had hired me so that he could convert me, and he certainly tried—part of my job was to sit at his desk and listen to him, seemingly for hours, discourse on what was wrong with the world—

and there was plenty wrong with it. When Tully eventually retired to California he was elected Chairman of the Board of the Association. A year later he informed me by letter that unless the Association agreed not to advertise in or make available for sale the liberal Catholic magazine, *Commonweal,* which had just endorsed Adlai E. Stevenson for president, he would resign. Fortunately, but not surprisingly, the other members of the Board of the Association agreed with me that such an ultimatum was unacceptable, and John Tully severed his connection with the organization he had founded.

Through the years the Association enjoyed, or suffered from, depending on your point of view, the services of a number of unusual people, but none more unusual than some of the group that greeted me when I first arrived. There was a woman known as "Bugs" to the rest of the staff, who firmly believed that the end of the world was nigh and smuggled literature on the subject from her desk to sometimes gullible, sometimes frightened visitors. The high point of our relationship came when she screamed at me in a voice that could be heard throughout the block, "Major, you're not in the Army now!" I forget the cause of her anger, but I do remember that we parted company the same day. There was another woman who boasted that her brother was the *enfant terrible* of the Iowa *avant-garde.* Because I had some doubts about her qualifications, I looked up her application and noted that she boasted of having played second trombone in a small town Iowa symphony orchestra.

Most of the women on our small staff were very pious and whenever there was no one to wait on customers in the bookshop, I had to bang on the door of the ladies' room where they frequently assembled to pray. Among the two or three men on the staff who did work was John Drahos, the superintendent of the shipping room, but when I asked him to describe his duties, he told me he was far too busy but might be able to talk to me the following week. I resolved he wouldn't be there the following week, but he was still present (as Sales Director) 37 years later. He really was not that way, but the managers had come and gone so quickly he had decided not to waste his time until he was sure one would stay. John Drahos has earned a secure place in the lore of Thomas More. Among other tales, he is remembered for fulfilling a suggestion that he tactfully handle the problem of a sales clerk with bad breath. He told the man, "Here's a dollar—go out and buy some mouthwash. You stink like a billy goat." To a job applicant who timidly inquired about the salary, he thundered, "We never discuss salary until after you are hired."

But John Drahos is perhaps proudest of his role as the seeker-out and bouncer of a free-loading priest (no longer with us) who managed to turn up regularly at Thomas More activities; using his Roman collar as a passport he would talk his way past the ticket-takers and ensconce himself in a front row seat. At Thomas More receptions, to which he was never invited, he was always first in the food and drink line. John's personal crusade to frustrate the good father's deadhead efforts finally became a bitter feud, ending only when the cheapskate left the priesthood, an action causing no sorrow at Thomas More.

One of our veteran staff members, who also worked full-time as a Pullman conductor, handled a variety of duties, including answering complaints. His favorite letter to priests who might complain of service began, "Dear Father: We know you are impeccable. . . ." (Some of his correspondents denounced him for being sarcastic, but he wasn't.) During Lent and Advent, he chose this admonition for all dissatisfied customers, "Let us not cross swords during this holy season." In later life he suffered from both loss of hearing and a jealous and suspicious wife. From time to time the wife would call and would not accept the excuse that her husband was in the men's room but would insist that he be brought to the phone immediately. His hearing problem intensified until he was forced to get a hearing aid, but he was very careful not to take it home at the end of the day or during vacations so he would not have to listen to his wife's harangues, he told us.

I refuse to speculate about the reason but toilets seemed always a problem at Thomas More. In an earlier location, one of our toilets regularly erupted, somewhat like Old Faithful geyser. I well remember the day a "real nun" (that is, one wearing a habit) came screaming out of the washroom shaking her soaking attire like a dog who had just come out of a lake, and directing a good deal of unnunlike language at the staff. Another time a nun stopped one of the clerks in the bookshop and said, "I wish to report there is a man in the women's room." Said the clerk, "On the contrary, Sister, you were in the men's room." Then there was the time eminent Jesuit, entertainer, raconteur and busybody, Daniel A. Lord, came to our bookshop to lecture to an assembly of several hundred nuns. Unfortunately, the podium was located near the door of the toilets. When he informed us that he needed to use the facilities rather badly before his lecture, we showed him the way to the men's room.

However, just as he was about to open the toilet door, 400 nuns burst into enthusiastic applause. He paused, and you could almost hear a sigh as he closed the door and proceeded to lecture. He disappeared immediately after the lecture, not even waiting for refreshments. Not many months later there was news of his death and I always wondered whether we might unwittingly have contributed to his demise.

At one time we sponsored a lecture by the eminent English historian, Christopher Dawson. It was held in the grand ballroom of a nearby hotel—unfortunately a room far too large, since Mr. Dawson had long ago passed his prime. Even at his best, it was difficult to hear or understand him. No one in the audience, to our knowledge, grasped more than a few words of what proved to be a tedious and boring lecture. My problem, however, occurred before the lecture when I was leading a group of distinguished guests, including several women, one a prominent publisher, from the speaker's assembly room to the grand ballroom. On the way I remembered that I had forgotten to visit the men's room and mindless of my entourage, proceded to do so, only to look around and discover that 20 men and women had followed me into that male sanctuary. The gentleman who was using the facility at the moment was more surprised than pleased.

Every bookshop, of course, attracts some odd types but we thought that our bookshop attracted more than its share. There was a man who appeared several times and demanded to be shown to his office—his uncle had died, and had willed the Thomas More Association to him. He was ready to take over. Even the police could not persuade him that we were not defrauding him of his inheritance. There was also a regular browser we called "the tapper" because in addition to looking for books that appealed to him, his obsession required that he tap on the shoulder of everyone in the bookshop, customer and clerk. We grew to accept his habit, but many of our patrons did not take kindly to it.

There was also the woman who turned up at a lecture by Father Patrick Peyton and tried to sell rosaries to the audience. When we asked her to desist, she prophesied in a loud voice that God would send an atom bomb to destroy us all. (Father Peyton is renowned, at least by me, for his call one day: "Danny boy," he said, "I know you're using my book in your Thomas More Book Club. While I was offering my mass this morning, it occurred to me to ask you as a friend of Our Lady what discount you got from the publisher.")

In addition to lectures and symposia, we also sponsored autographing parties—encouraged by publishers for the sake of an author's ego and with little expectation of selling books. Most of our autographing parties were disasters, but possibly the worst fiasco was a feature of our 10th anniversary celebration—actually, as we discovered sometime later, it was either our 9th or 11th. I can't remember which. Our advertised attraction was Gerald Brennan, the author of a series of perfectly dreadful juveniles. Although we widely promoted the affair, it was soon obvious that the "crowd" consisted of a handful of old ladies who had come in out of the cold. To keep Father Brennan from realizing the truth, we adopted emergency measures: a large crew of high school boys working in our shipping room that Saturday morning were told to put on their coats, walk around the block to the front entrance and pretend they were interested spectators. Unfortunately, the boys looked like (and probably were) dead enders—they slouched in their chairs, ground out cigarette butts on the floor and otherwise disgraced us. The high point in absurdity was reached when Father Brennan's publisher, Frank Bruce, made an unscheduled speech to tell how inspired he had been by the sight of these young lovers of literature coming to the autographing party on a day when they might be playing basketball with their friends.

We had publicity successes as well as failures, the most satisfying being the time we bested our (usually) friendly competitor Nina Polcyn, the proprietor of St. Benet's Shop, an outgrowth of Bishop Bernard Sheil's CYO. St. Benet's was the darling of the Catholic establishment which barely tolerated Thomas More.

There was much excitement in Catholic circles when Ms. Polcyn announced that the grand opening of a second bookshop in the suburb of Wilmette was to feature the personal appearance of no less a personage than Cardinal Samuel Stritch, Archbishop of Chicago, who would impart his official blessing. When the great day arrived, the Cardinal's limousine drove up to the new St. Benet's and a large crowd of well-wishers applauded as Ms. Polcyn opened the door of the car—only to have Dan Herr, beloved president of the Thomas More Association, step forth. (At the time I was writing a profile of Cardinal Stritch and I suggested it would be more convenient for him if I interviewed him enroute instead of in his office—en route, for example, to the opening of St. Benet's. Not suspecting my motives, he agreed. I regret that I do not have a picture of that glorious occasion, particularly a picture of Nina Polcyn at that proud moment.)

Of course there was another, far more important side
to life at Thomas More, and it was far from uneventful.
For many hectic and exuberant years almost everything
we attempted seemed to be successful. Then our life
changed radically as a result of the aftermath of the Second Vatican Council. Pundits decreed that a transition
period was inevitable and that we were on our way to
a far greater and more effective church. That still may
be true, but it's hard to tell when the transition period
will be over and what the new Church will be. In any
event, the Association which—post-Tully, at least—had
directed its activities toward the liberal Catholic found
that many liberal Catholics were the first to decide that
the Church was no longer for them. Many nuns, who
were the nucleus of the Catholic reading public, discovered needs other than books for their time and money.
As interest in our activities declined, we found it necessary to close our bookshop, to reduce our staff, to
eliminate pensions, to trim salaries and vacations, to
curtail many activities, and to move from our proud loop
location to a near-northside building that perhaps had
never seen better days. We became accustomed to prim-
itive restrooms, rats and mice, floods and dirt and similar discomforts. I realized for the first time why some
slum-dwellers give up trying to keep their homes clean.
In our new offices we soon acclimated ourselves to a
fair share of dirt and grime. I think Dickens might have
felt at home visiting us, appreciating that we had recap-
tured the spirit of his novels. If he was like our other
visitors, however, we would not expect him a second
time.

There is a happy ending to this sad, sad story, but before I reveal it, I should focus on those who made it possible, although this recital may sound like an acceptance

speech at an Oscar Night. Andrew Greeley (unlike another who will be nameless) has been a loyal and supportive friend for more than 30 years and we proudly continue to publish at least one book of his each year— though top publishers are vying for his works since he became a habitue of the *New York Times* best-seller list. Thomas More has also benefited mightily by advice, grants and friendship from the Claretian Fathers and Brothers and can never repay an incredible fairy godmother who insists on remaining anonymous. And through the years, even when the going was toughest, the Directors of the Association never wavered in their support. They are: Robert Lee Berner (who quickly established the critical distinction between the prerogatives of the Board and those of Management), Robert E. Burns (of *U.S. Catholic* fame), Walter J. Cummings (Chief Judge, Seventh Court of Appeals), Roger J. Kiley (Cook County Chancery Court Judge) and Candida Lund (the wise and witty Chancellor of Rosary College who is also a valued Association author).

Thanks to these and our other benefactors—we had to swallow our pride and for the first time engage in a fund drive—good fortune returned to Thomas More and we were able to leave our office slum and move to clean, bright offices in a beautifully rehabbed building. There is only one drawback: we occupy the floor beneath a famous ballet school and many afternoons our floor is well shaken by flying feet. Although rehearsals for "Swan Lake" are rather pleasant, "Rodeo" performances are a problem. But after our previous sufferings, no one seems to mind too much.

And finally, whatever the Thomas More Association has accomplished—and I suspect there are those who would shout "damn little"—some credit should be given to a peerless octet: Todd Brennan, the President of the Association; Joel Wells, the Editor-in-Chief; Business Manager Joan Karwat; John and Jerry Drahos, now wallowing in retirement; Veronica Droszcz, Sales Manager; John Sprague, Promotion Director and chief problem-solver who, after 15 years is still considered "the new young man"; and, if I may be immodest, me.

No story about my life in Chicago would be credible if I did not relate at least some of my experiences with Eppie Lederer, known to millions as Ann Landers.

I first met Mrs. Lederer through her daughter Margo Howard, a talented writer whose biography of her mother, *Eppie,* is a worthy portrait of this fascinating and beautiful woman. Through the can't-remember-how-many years that I have known Eppie our relationship has never been calm and has often been tempestuous. A typical low point—or high point, depending on your perspective—occurred when I finally inveigled her into seeing my favorite comic movie, *Where's Poppa,* promising her at least a bellylaugh a minute. Unfortunately, I had forgotten that many episodes in it might charitably be described as ribald or even raunchy. And, like Queen Victoria before her, Eppie does not find this kind of humor amusing. Halfway through the movie when the mother, played by Ruth Gordon, attempts to frighten her son's latest romantic interest by deprecating the size of his penis, Eppie let out a cry of outrage and rushed out of the theater, with me trailing her, vainly trying to explain from several paces behind that it was just good clean fun.

Then there was the time I sent Eppie a small St. Nicholas Day gift—a lump of coal which is traditionally given on that day to "bad little girls." I did not anticipate that in unwrapping it she would smudge coal all over her hands, face, new dress and a group of letters her secretary had just delivered. Her note of thanks—she is very punctillious about thank-you notes—exuded a certain degree of frigidity.

When my brother was recuperating in a Chicago hospital Eppie selected the coldest and windiest night of the year to visit him. When I suggested we take a taxi home from the hospital, she overrode my suggestion, implying that I was soft and spoiled. She waved away the taxi I had secured with great difficulty and announced bravely "We can make it." But as we struggled through the blinding snow and whipping winds, my valiant companion began to doubt that we would reach her home alive. Then a miracle came to pass—a second taxi appeared, but as Eppie ran toward it she slipped and fell hip deep into a snowbank. I am proud that I limited my comment to: "There is a God!"

Eppie appreciates my cooking talents—or she is using the Tom Sawyer fence-whitewashing technique on me. My meat loaf is one of her delights, as are my sweet and sour salad dressing and my spaghetti sauce. Desserts, however, are the way to her heart—she finds anything chocolate irresistible. With rice pudding a close second. One day I slaved for hours preparing what I hoped would be a particularly spectacular version. She took one taste of the concoction and said, tactfully, "It's awful." Unfortunately, the other guests agreed and finally even I had to admit she was right. With her help I poured the whole damn pudding down the garbage disposal.

We tend to disagree about restaurants—for example, she refuses to ever again visit my favorite Chinese restaurant, admittedly short on decor but, in my opinion, high in the quality of its food. It is owned and dominated by a harridan my friends and I fondly call the Dragon Lady. When Eppie decided to indulge me she called the restaurant for a reservation. The conversation went something like this. Eppie: "This is Ann Landers." Dragon Lady, as she hangs up: "She no here." On the second call, Eppie tried again: "This is Ann Landers, the newspaper columnist." Dragon Lady: "I no read newspapers." Eppie: "I would like to make a reservation." Dragon Lady: "You come, no seats, you wait. You come, seats, you sit." When we arrived at the half-empty restaurant Eppie was impressed with neither the ambience nor the food and declared that she would try any restaurant once—and once was enough for "this joint."

Between our arguments, Eppie was been a warm and good friend. She has helped me through surgery and illnesses; she has listened sympatheticaly to my troubles (as long as I kept my recitals short), and has been the source of a great deal of cheer and joy.

9) The Critic

By far the most prestigious and influential of the many Thomas More activities is our magazine, *The Critic*. It had a curious beginning. Soon after John Tully founded Thomas More he decided he must do his part to combat immoral books and to promote "Catholic books" which have always needed help. (The publication of Thomas Merton's *Seven Storey Mountain* in 1948 heralded the first public recognition of the genre.) Tully started a magazine and called it *Books on Trial;* if there was any doubt about his editorial approach, the courtroom logo on the cover made the focus clear. There were book reviews but the publicized feature of *Books on Trial* were the charts which rated current books, mostly from a moral viewpoint. These charts were reprinted and distributed to parishes to enable Catholic readers to keep up with what amounted to a Legion of Decency for literature. Books were rated under such categories as: "Unfavorable"; "Offensive or Objectionable in whole or in part"; "Disapproved"; "Doubtful merit"; "Why bother reading"; "Somewhat questionable". *Dragonseed* by Pearl Buck was found both unfavorable and offensive; *The White Tower* by James Ramsey Olman was termed offensive because of "inexcusable and objectionable language"; both *The Wayward Bus* by John Steinbeck and *Joseph the Provider* by Thomas Mann were rated unfavorable and objectionable and were disapproved. Unfortunately, many of the books that merited approval were never heard from again.

By the time I came along, the morality charts were proving troublesome. Soon they disappeared and few readers seemed to care. We changed the title of the magazine to *The Critic* to announce our new approach, a move somewhat startling to older subscribers. *The Critic* under the inspired editorship of Joel Wells, later assisted by Todd Brennan was a far cry from *Books on Trial* but the earlier magazine made *The Critic* possible.

The roster of *Critic* authors is a glorious one and includes Andrew Greeley, Martin Luther King, Thomas Merton, Francois Mauriac, Graham Greene, Evelyn Waugh, Sean O'Faolain, Nelson Algren (when he first visited us and Joel Wells introduced me, he said, "I've heard of you," and I replied, "I've heard of you, too," to which he said, "That was a dumb remark of mine"— and I agreed), Brian Friel, Anthony Burgess, Agatha Christie, Tom Wolfe, Martin Marty, William F. Buckley, Joyce Carol Oates, T.S. Eliot, Arnold Toynbee, Arthur Koestler, John Shea, Flannery O'Connor—and others equally celebrated, many who were being published for the first time, as well as representatives of the handful of literate high churchmen.

Looking back at more than 30 years of *The Critic,* I am somewhat startled by our impudence, perhaps even arrogance, and our courage at a time when the Catholic press by and large was fettered. Now and then our articles precipitated controversy: notably, articles by Ivan Illich and John L. McKenzie, which brought down upon both of them the wrath of the Vatican, and a progressive—for that time—view of censorship by the eminent Jesuit theologian, John Courtney Murray. When Father Murray's article caused a tizzy among conservative churchmen, the Chicago Chancery Office threatened us with a severe reprimand, only to learn to its chagrin that for the first and only time in our history, we had obtained an Imprimatur for the article. Through the years, most of the innumerable gripe letters and phone calls, however, came as a result of our cartoons and, as we admitted in a "final" editorial when *The Critic* recessed publication, "It could be argued that there were times when we went too far—a cartoon cover which showed a corpulent bishop (identifiable, it was claimed) trying to squeeze in a church door with a sign reading 'Extra Wide Load' attached to his back." There were few features of Catholic life, private and institutional, that sooner or later our cartoons did not satirize. That two of our regular cartoonists also appeared in *Playboy* did not endear us to conservative readers; nor did the editor's stock answer to these complainers, "But how did you discover that?" (I must note that the only time *The Critic* ran an editorial—we condemned the Vietnam War—not one reader complained.)

One series that offended more readers than it pleased was "Catholic Classics Revisited" by Joel Wells. In one essay he discussed at length *Little Nelly of Holy God* by Margaret Gibbons, a biography of a saintly little girl in Ireland which recorded her utterances in the "authentic babytalk in which she delivered them." Poor Nelly lived in an orphanage from the age of three years, nine months (she "bore the fatal spores of T.B. contacted from—as Nelly always called her—'my dead mommy' "). The unique flavor of the book can be seen in this anecdote: Nelly was no "plaster saint." She could be naughty, as she was one night. One of the nuns (she called them her "Modders") reprimanded poor Nelly and told her she should make an Act of Contrition for what she had done.

Nelly immediately dropped to her knees and prayed, "Holy Dod, I am berry sorry for teeping de girls late for supper; please forgib me and make a good child and bless me and my Modders." When Nelly was dying, the convent in which she was living was having financial problems and one of the Sistes reminded her that she would soon be with God and suggested she ask God to send them money. Replied Nelly, "Him knows and dat's enough."

Another "Catholic Classic" to win the attention of Joel Wells was *Father William Doyle, S.J.—A Spiritual Study* by Alfred O'Rahilly. Father Doyle, also Irish, was known for "living a life of secret mortification and ceaseless prayer while turning a lovable, even boisterous exterior to the world." Among his privations was a practice of arising at 3:00 in the morning on cold winter nights and standing up to his neck in a nearby pond praying for sinners. Father Willy's greatest triumph, however, was in becoming "the master of the ejaculation"—that is of short prayers or pious aspirations. We learn that "Father Willy began with a mere 10,000 per day in 1911, but by 1915 this had grown to 25,000, if possible 10,000 before lunch. Then by 1916, when he was engaged in service as a chaplain for an Irish regiment in France, he realized with horror how many opportunities he had missed by not ejaculating in his early years and noted that 'at the rate of 10,000 a day for 15 years, this would amount to 54 million. I have promised Him to pay this back, counting only anything above the usual 50,000 a day.' He soon hit 100,000 but began to experience trouble and discouragement, 'for I must watch every spare moment of the day to perform my penance.' But he overcame this dark night of the ejaculation by striking a bargain with Jesus 'to give me a soul for every 1,000 made over the daily 100,000.' Thus in 1917 he hit his all-time high of 120,000 ejaculations in a single day."

Not surprisingly, Father Willy was a great admirer of Little Nelly and after visiting her grave decided on even greater mortification, such as "rolling in nettles at every opportunity and cutting Jesus' name into his bosom with a penknife." He not only wore a hair shirt but improved on it by heating the shirt in a stove before putting it on. (He was delighted that the hot shirt caused "such lovely blisters.") One day he even achieved the ultimate sacrifice by giving up penance as a penance for 24 hours —"That hurt the most," we learn.

From the early days of *The Critic,* I contributed a regular column, "Stop Pushing." (The title, "Stop Pushing," was a reference to an editorial slogan in that fabulous New York newspaper *PM* which was opposed to people pushing other people around.) Regular, that is, except for three issues when I dropped out just to prove that there would be a flood of letters protesting my absence. Unfortunately, even I could not describe two letters as a flood, so I returned somewhat chastened. I had a similar humiliating experience when I decided to take life a little easier and reprint some of my columns. When I began to search for columns to reprint, I had to admit that the early columns seemed jejune and strained—I like to think I improved in my later years.

There were no limitations, except the laws against libel and obscenity, and in general I think my subject matter could be described as truly catholic—I usually wrote about the last things that had irritated me. I was and still am easily irritated. I suppose these quotations from my columns could be considered typical:

"In all the blather foamed up by experts about the New Generation, or whatever you may choose to call them, no one yet has pointed out the most distinguishing characteristic of the breed: they have not been taught or are too lazy to flush the toilet."

* * *

"Nineteen-sixty-four may well go down in history as the year Michael Novak discovered 'sex.' At least he has proved that there is no subject which cannot be dulled by too much writing about it."

* * *

"I like to recall a story told me by Knopf editor Herbert Weinstock, a friend of and editor for Sigrid Undset. Near Ms. Undset's home in the mountains of Norway lived a beloved and saintly hermit. She heard that he was dying and made one final request—to see a naked woman before he died. Ms. Undset, although in poor health herself, struggled up the mountain to the hermit's home, opened her coat and granted him his last wish. (It should be noted that Ms. Undset weighed in the neighborhood of 300 pounds, so it is doubtful that the hermit was troubled by concupiscence in his last moments."

* * *

"Since the Council, our new jet set of theologians have been so busy jetting about the world from symposium to symposium, from lecture to lecture, from meeting to meeting, that they have had little or no time to practice their craft. In a day when creative thinking on the part of the theologian is needed more than ever before, we find our theologians so occupied with celebrity activities that they have had to all but give up theology. (There is a notorious case of one great theologian who early in the game was shot out of obscurity and hasn't had time to have an original thought since.)"

* * *

"Memories of the Catholic Press: Generally the various panels and workshops at Catholic Press Association conventions were not well attended. The one exception—and what an exception—that I can recall was a lecture by Monsignor Thomas Fitzgerald, head of the National Office for Decent Literature (NODL). Fitzgerald, known affectionately as 'dirty books Fitzgerald' to distinguish him from his brother, also a Monsignor, was a nice guy who had not asked for his assignment but tried his best. His talk on printed filth brought out the biggest crowd of its kind I ever saw at a CPA convention and, when he began to read from the books to show the depths of degradations to which supposedly respectable publishers as well as pornographers had gone, the crowd grew even bigger until finally the only conventiongoer not present was the newspaperman who always spent his conventions in the hotel bar. It was most edifying to see the concern shown by members of the Catholic Press, lay, clerical and religious. Obviously, they could not condemn immoral literature unless they were exposed to it and they seemed willing to make the sacrifice for their readers. Let us bow our heads in gratitude. (All right, so I was there, too—in the front row, if you must know.)"

* * *

"I have been recently pinioned by Paul H. Hallett in the *National Catholic Register* who calls me 'a respected leader of Catholoic "liberalism" for the past 15 years'— which, I fear, is not intended as a compliment. He has also decided I am 'Hegel-like,' whatever that means. (It's my year for glory: in *The Wanderer,* Joseph T. Gill calls me an 'elder statesman of Catholic liberalism' and, hold your breath, 'one of the point men in the *avante garde.*') But the object of all this is not to preen myself but to quote Mr. Hallett's conclusion: 'These infallible inter-pretations of progress in Catholic teaching show that it is impossible for any development in the legitimate teaching of Catholic faith and morals to be contrary to what has previously been taught. This includes, for ex-ample, the determinations of the Church on birth con-trol and the invalidity of female ordination." I presume in the same category Mr. Hallett would include the Church's one-time teachings on slavery, usury and the sun revolving around the earth, to name but three."

* * *

"I suppose there are grave problems with unlimited freedom and certainly some measures must be taken to protect so-called innocent children from pornogra-phers. What can be done to protect adults is far more complex and, to my mind, far less certain. Perhaps all that I am saying is that the busybodies who devote their lives to restraining sexual permissiveness may at best have too little to do and at worst are desperately in need of psychiatric counselling. Looking at the blundering censors of the past, particularly in my lifetime, I would judge that whatever good they have accomplished has been more than offset by their attempts to limit basic freedom and by their general stupidities. There must be better ways to solve a problem. And, I suggest, there may just possibly be other areas of human activity more worthy of attention."

* * *

"I submit, quietly, as is my wont, that, all-American as it may be, Thanksgiving is a disgusting holiday—a paen to over-abundance and a symbol of the greatest of American vices. This is the day we dedicate to the gross art of over-eating and any serious relationship with the traditional meaning, if any—to my mind, the Puritans were simply indulging in better-than-the-Indians triumphalism—has long been lost. Despite efforts to weld religious significance into our gastronomic orgy, the holiday consists entirely of one gargantuan meal, preliminaries for which begin many days ahead—the number of days dependent upon the culinary skill and the financial resources of the hostess. From early morning, final preparations go forward for *the* Meal. When the gluttons have at last had their fill, the male members of the family (with the possible exception of those whose wives have been liberated) rouse themselves from their stupor long enough to turn on TV for their quota of football games while the cooks and helpers clean up the awful mess."

* * *

(After a survey of one week's issue of 80 diocesan newspapers) "Among the subjects found worthy of comments by editors in the issue I perused were: smut (smother it), Bobby Baker (don't smother him), over-organized Catholics (perhaps), birth control (against), voting at eighteen (against), poverty (against), Khrushchev's birthday (noncommittal), capital punishment (against), our new bishop (for), earthquakes (against), violence (against), fair housing (for), Boy's Club Week (for), collegiate orgy (against), alcoholism (against), Cardinal Koenig (for), nuclear warfare (against), Senator Thurmond (against), Knights of Columbus (for), crime in New York (against), L.B.J. as a preacher (for), Governor Wallace (against)."

* * *

"There is a new book *What Can I Do for Christ* by Clementine Lenta purporting to show young Catholics the wide variety of apostolic activity available to them. Among the activities, the Marylike Crusade. Among the Crusade projects—but you wouldn't believe it unless I quoted: 'There is another important thing to remember in the matter of our appearance and that is that no matter how modest and attractive a dress may be, the entire effect can be destroyed in an instant by the wearing of an immodestly styled bra. Modest bras are difficult to obtain in local stores. The *Marylike Fashion Center,* therefore, provides a real service in furnishing modest bras. These are available in sizes 32 through 40 and are priced at just 12.00. Since most bra styles now on the market are definitely not something which Mary would approve, there is a real need for girls and women to interest others in the *Marylike* bra.' "

"Another barrier between the bishops and the people is the Establishment's reluctance to abandon monarchial trappings. It is very difficult for Americans to seriously accept costumes which would not be out of place at a masquerade party but seem precious and pitiful in the real world. Fortunately, most bishops have at least eliminated the practice of ring kissing but other similarly outdated practices (peccadilloes?) are still in force."

* * *

"What stirred the Catholics of Davenport, Iowa, during the final days of March 1980? The plight of the hostages in Iran? E.R.A.? Inflation? The Soviet invasion of Afghanistan? The Hans Kung controversy? Crime in the streets? Sorry, the answer is none of the above. What exercised the good people of Iowa as Spring burst forth was the printing of an 'angry expletive' in the diocesan weekly, *The Catholic Messenger.* I am embarrassed to admit that although I read the article, the controversial word made no impression on me and thus I cannot be sure that it was the good old stand-by 'shit,' but from circumstantial evidence I suspect that it was. As a result of phone calls and irate letters from readers (one Helen Hembreider piously proclaimed, 'Surely four-letter words should not come from the mouth or the pen of a priest'), the editor, in a full-length, double-column editorial, attempted to justify the suspension of the rule 'against printing vulgarity.' He explained that the horrendous word appeared in a personal journal of a hospital chaplain who 'felt lonely, frustrated and angry' after 'a long day spent ministering to dying and fearful patients and their families.' There followed a somewhat tortured recounting of how the decision to print *that* word was arrived at by the editors. It makes you feel good all over, doesn't it, to realize that people still care?"

* * *

"Through the years I have collected stories from retreats and sermons. Not intentionally. It's just that I can't help being pious. All too typical of my memorable collection is a story from a Jesuit high school retreat master, Father Henry, about a young Catholic boy who was struck by lightning while lying with a prostitute. At the post mortem, doctors found etched on his chest the words, 'I have sinned.' My favorite story of all (courtesy of the late Fulton J. Sheen) is about a young nobleman who lusted after a harlot. She promised to grant him her favors (as we used to say) only if he would bring her the heart of his mother. He jumped on his horse, rode to his home town, unsheathed his knife, cut out his mother's heart and hung it from his saddle. Rushing back in anticipation of the pleasures to come, he was thrown to the ground when his horse stumbled. From the mother's heart came the cry, 'Are you hurt, son?' "

* * *

Not even a brief history of *The Critic* could ignore the tizzy caused by my comments on Cardinal Spellman's potboiler, *The Foundling.* An advance copy arrived shortly before our deadline and the editor asked me if I would do a quick review. Because I was in a charitable mood, it seemed to me useless to blast the book—it obviously had no literary merit and I assumed (wrongly) the Cardinal realized this. I started my review this way, "Let's begin by admitting that Cardinal Spellman is no Graham Greene or Evelyn Waugh and that he has not produced the great Catholic novel." I charitably proceeded to say that the book was unpretentious and had charm and warmth. More than a year later we received a telephone request from the New York Chancery Office for a copy of that issue. Less than a week after, an official letter arrived from Cardinal Samuel Stritch, the Archbishop of Chicago, condemning me for daring to compare a prince of the church with authors who have "tried to introduce certain materialistic, ultra-modern styles and techniques. . . . In the art of literature there is in our times apparent a certain idiom which is as wrong for Catholic authors and literary people as the styles and techniques condemned by the Holy See." The only saving feature of the episode was that I happened to attend a banquet a night later where Cardinal Stritch went out of his way to see me and say, "Don't pay any attention to that letter. I had to write it."

On rereading my review, I have decided I was too kind—the book is a stinker.

Although it was a rare book review that caused controversy, there was seldom an issue without at least one article that brought forth letters, often bitter letters. *Critic* articles ranged from satire to spiritual meditation, from denunciation of censorship to a plea for another Vatican Council. (What *The Critic* seldom published, because of Editor Wells' trumpeted prejudice, was poetry—in fact, for many years the masthead carried the line, "Unsolicited poetry is resented.") Among the

more memorable articles, because of the original and
provocative content as well as the intense reaction, were:
"The Vanishing Clergyman" by Ivan Illich, "Hang Your
Head, Tom Dooley" by Nicholas Von Hoffman, "Black
Agony" by Martin Luther King, "Women as 'Niggers' of
the Church" by Sister Albertus Magnus, "Is Catholic Sexual Teaching Coming Apart" by Andrew Greeley (who
contributed far more than his share of controversial articles), "Visiting Porno Movies" by Todd Brennan; "The
Other Side of Despair" by Thomas Merton; "The Em-
blems and Proofs of Power" by Nelson Algren; "Conscience and Authority" by Cardinal John Wright; and
others equally stimulating. Between our cartoons and
controversial articles, our mail was usually heavy with
strong letters of protest.

What our detractors fervently hoped and prayed for
finally came about. The Association could no longer
carry the very heavy burden of subsidizing *The Critic*.
For three years we changed the *Critic* into a striking
8-page newsletter which, looking backwards now, was
underrated by readers and the staff. Because even that
proved a drain on the Association, we finally declared
a recess. As we announced in our "farewell" issue, we
were finally done in by the seeming dwindling of the
liberal Catholic readers who had supported *The Critic*
through the years: "They were among the first to decide
that the promise and expectations roused by Vatican
II were coming to little that was new and, for a variety
of reasons, signaled by, but not summed up by, the birth
control encyclical *Humanae Vitae*, drifted away from further intellectual interest in the Church. There was no
one to replace them and *Critic* circulation began a steady
plummet."

But *The Critic* was just too good to die quietly. In the Fall of 1985 the fourth incarnation of the magazine came into being (under the editorship of John Sprague) with the hope that it could carry on, in a new format, the glorious traditions of the past.

Obviously, a story to be continued.

10) Lo, The Poor Bachelor

ALTHOUGH I have not previously confessed in these pages that I am a bachelor, astute readers may already have guessed my shame. Unlike the old days, being a bachelor is now almost a sign of ignominy. Once bachelors were considered kindly and beloved and an asset to any family: loyal, dependable, helpful—the family bachelor was the first to be called in every emergency from baby-sitting to life-saving.

Today the bachelor is hounded and persecuted. It seems to be the general belief that almost all bachelors are either gay or child molesters, or both, and that among their ranks can be found an indecent proportion of voyeurs and flashers. Because he is not married, a bachelor's sex life, or lack thereof, is suspect. No sensible modern parent would consider allowing a bachelor to baby-sit. After all, if he is normal, why isn't he married? (I must note that the image of the bachelor has not been helped by the thousands of priests who have deserted celibacy for marriage; this trend has only confirmed widely held prejudices.) Rumors and suspicions about bachelors' sexual proclivities are so pervasive, fed as they are by pop-psychologists, that the bachelors themselves have begun to believe they are an abnormal species. After all, so many people can't be wrong.

I have discovered that the wives of my male friends are in the first line of attack. If circumstances they cannot change force wives to tolerate the temporary presence of bachelors, they solve the problem neatly by scurrying around and finding the most ineligible of their unmarried girlfriends in an attempt to make a match.

Usually these fiendish moves succeed only in instantly removing the terrified bachelor from the premises. However, if the poor guy falls for Miss Wallflower of 1932, that's a coup—another bachelor has been trapped and milady has preserved her castle against the invading bachelor forces. But even if that particular problem does not arise, any bachelor who thinks he will maintain close ties with male friends, once they marry, is naive. A wife sees in a bachelor a threat to her happy wedded life; her husband will envy the bachelor's independence and long for the good old days, he may even rejoin the old gang. Then it's back to carousing, gambling and God knows what—the female's image of the bachelor life. The solution, most wives decide, is to freeze the friendship as soon as possible after the honeymoon when husbands are still pliable.

Bachelors, however, are always willing to help married men. Some couples have been known to be less than happy at least once during the course of their marriage. At such a time, when a husband is underappreciated or mistreated, he desperately wants someone to confide in, someone to advise him how to deal with injustice. Who better in this hour of need than his bachelor friend who is bound to be sympathetic and whose advice will surely prove helpful and objective? Even here, however, the bachelor is vulnerable. Sooner or later most husbands and wives settle their differences. Not infrequently, a bigmouth husband tells his wife what the well-meaning bachelor advised and all hell breaks loose.

Speaking for beleaguered bachelors, I would like to submit that, contrary to the belief of all nonbachelors, we are not loaded with money. In fact, most of us can barely scrape along—the financial demands on us are so heavy. Contemplate, if you will, the cost of wedding presents year after year. From early manhood till death mercifully releases us from an obligation that is more inevitable than taxes, we bachelors are expected to give generous, even munificent gifts at Christmas, birthdays, anniversaries and every other trumped-up occasion. One of the neatest tricks is to snare a bachelor as a godfather (only a churl could refuse such an honor). What the duffer does not realize until too late is that he has made a commitment for hundreds of dollars in gifts, from birth through graduations to marriage. For all of this outpouring of money what can he hope for in return? He will be among the fortunate if, once he turns off the gift faucet, he rates a Christmas card at the nursing home.

The occasions upon which gifts are expected to be lavished are as numerous as the outstretched hands waiting for the payoff. When a bachelor is invited over for dinner in a burst of pity on the part of a married friend who is probably suffering from the gout and can't get out of the house, he is not only expected to exhibit the gratitude of a puppy for years to come, not only to bring a suitable gift for the children *and* the parents, but soon after to reciprocate by inviting the couple out to dinner. Not just a plain dinner at some ordinary restaurant, mind you, but a real blowout at the fanciest place in town.

The good old bachelor is always an easy mark for a touch, too. Are you a little short this week? Did you lose too much in that poker game? Did your helpmate forget herself and overindulge at the supermarket? Does she need a permanent ever so badly right this minute even though it's not budgeted until next month? No problem—just drop a word to the good old bachelor victim.

Not for him the excuse that he's strapped. How could he possibly be broke? He has no expenses worth talking about. Dismiss the thought that he pays more taxes, that every worthwhile and nonworthwhile cause in town expects him to be at the head of their list of contributors, that relatives and friends are a continual drain on his financial resources, what with gifts and one thing and another, that he must buy more expensive clothes and dress better than the rest because he is expected to be a style leader—but only bachelors can appreciate the extent of our financial harassment.

Gifts are but part of the problem involved with the children of married friends. Some bachelors I know argue that it is far better to sever the friendship before a friend becomes a father and inevitably a bore, relating the playful actions of his toddlers and later deploring the nefarious activities of his adolescents. Not for a moment do parents ask themselves if their bachelor friend is interested in an endless chronicle of the clever actions and sayings of their offspring. No, they just go on yakking about the kids until the poor bachelor turns into a real child-hater and is ultimately jailed for kicking defenseless children on the street, seemingly without provocation.

For years I have been crusading for the cause of bachelors. With very little success, I might add. There has even been a good deal of opposition to my crusade, the most virulent coming from my own colleague, Joel Wells (editor, homilist, aspiring novelist, parodist, spiritual writer, humorist, curmudgeon—choose one). He finally decided he could no longer take my mutterings in silence and presented me with this retort:

"Bachelors are the crybabies of the Western World.

We married couples are sick unto our second mortgages with hearing their puerile complaints which, compared to the difficulties and hardships gladly and silently borne by married people sound like a politician complaining of an ingrown toenail in a military hospital filled with wounded soldiers.

"The psychiatrist who said that all bachelors need psychiatric help was simply propounding the obvious. Most of them have never recovered from the cataclysmic experience of being born and finding out that they would have to share the world with other people. It is true that it swells the bachelor's already king-sized ego to think that all unmarried women are out to trap him, but this is not the real reason why he eludes marriage. Who needs marriage when one is already deeply involved in a flaming romance with oneself?

"The few bachelors I know are holdovers from the Elizabethan age, dandies dedicated to the frivolities of life. As far as I can tell they do not carry lace handkerchiefs in their sleeves, or use snuff, but they do indulge in all the modern equivalents of these things from wearing silk underwear and monogrammed shirts, to driving expensive cars and having their hair cut by appointment. I am thinking of one bachelor in particular, Mr. Herr, well known to both of us, whose dedication to the comforts of life is almost mystic in its intensity.

"In this single classic specimen to which I have reference, one can observe all generic traits of the modern bachelor. He appoints himself elegantly; he dines in the finest places; he cannot abide children (though he considers himself an expert on their rearing); he twits husbands about their restricted freedom and baits wives by inviting husbands to poker parties and on fishing trips;

he moans continually about the inequity of the tax structure (exemptions, school taxes); he loves to complain about giving wedding presents and baby gifts, yet prides himself on giving more expensive presents than married people can afford to show that after all, *noblesse oblige;* he maintains a luxurious apartment which is kept at a high gloss by a maid and which is never, never sullied by childish hand or foot; and, because they obey him blindly, expecting nothing in return, he even keeps two cats.

"Observe one of his typical days. On a work day he rises at the heroically early hour of eight (eleven on Saturdays and Sundays), breakfasts on the elaborate pastries and imported ham which he purchased the evening before, takes a leisurely shower, and dons his custom-made clothes. At last about ten minutes until nine, he pets the cats, writes out a curt note to the maid informing her that she is *not* to dust the original paintings on the wall, and steps out the door and down the hall to the elevator. Oh, I forgot, before he leaves he calls the building's doorman to hail him a cab (he once gave his thumb a nasty wrench when trying to signal one for himself).

"Arriving at work fresh and unharried, he devotes most of his day to making life miserable for his married colleagues who are exhausted from their morning's struggle with children, garbage cans, snow-shovels, crowded public transportation, and the like. 'The trouble with you fellows,' he is fond of telling them, 'is that you don't plan your days like I do.' Shortly before closing time he will instruct his secretary to call and make reservations at his favorite restaurant, and if he is in the mood, see what theatre tickets are available. When he finally breezes home, he gathers up the day's papers and magazines, puts out some chopped chicken livers for the cats, turns on his stereo set, pours himself a refreshing drink, stretches out on his antique sofa (a masterpiece of opulent comfort originally designed for King Louis XIV but rejected by him as being too soft), and recovers from the rigors of the day.

"Yes, the bachelor's lot is a hard one. We commiserate with them; we turn our heads to weep, and weeping, at last our tears run dry, we cease to grieve—just as we have ceased to grieve at the passing of the dinosaur, the dodo bird, and all those creatures whose existence having become pointless, have passed into oblivion."

So much for the mutterings of a mean-spirited, envious cynic.

11) Dogs, Cats, Pigeons— Where Will It End?

WHILE I have no sympathy with those dregs of society who hate pets, I will admit that pet owners may be responsible in part for this intolerant state of mind. Said pet owners not being content to contain the enjoyment their little rascals bring them insist on telling all within hearing the cute doings of their four-legged loved ones. City dog walkers are particularly keen on showing off their pets in elevators, in lobbies and on the street— but not so keen on cleaning up after them. On the other hand, many singles and childless couples have adopted pets in self-defense; they need something to shut up proud parents or at least equalize the boredom—you spin your stories about your darling children and we will match you hour for hour with scintillating tales about our canine friends.

I have been pet-happy most of my days and if the rumor is true that nursing homes now permit pets I hope to continue that attachment into the future. I am told my family had pets before I came on this earth, most notably a pony and a goat. But by the time I arrived we had slimmed down to cats and dogs. The cats made little impression but I can recall two dogs: Bosco and Trixie. Bosco could charitably be called a "mixed breed" whose chief claim to fame was that he detested the sound of fireworks so prevalent in small towns before and on the 4th of July. He would disappear when the first firecracker was lighted near the end of June, not to turn up until a week later. When Bosco died, his place was taken by Trixie, a delightful fox terrier whose greatest virtue was patience. She would suffer costumes of all descriptions which I inflicted on her to celebrate holidays or to highlight family entertainments. She came to a sad end, however, because some contemptible neighbor poisoned her. About this time, I left Huron for school and had to forego the pleasure of pets until I came out of the Army in 1945.

After the War, I was living in Washington with my sister and her husband. In a fit of nostalgia, my sister and I decided a dog was needed to complete the household and although my brother-in-law had never known the joys of pet-owning, he agreed, and to the pound we went, coming home with a frisky German shepherd puppy which we named Yank. In a few months the lovable puppy grew into a monster with the body of a horse and the disposition of a mosquito. My sister at that time believed in all the fashionable theories of raising children and tested them on Yank. Although in a way this was fortunate since she learned the error of her theories and did not perpetuate them later on her family, the result was a dog whose favorite occupation (other than forcing me to cower in a corner whenever he charged into the room) was ripping through the screen door and chasing the mailman down the block. After a week of no mail and the threat of a law suit, we decided to present him to my brother, then the principal of a high school in Ohio. My brother's pastor did not take kindly to having a dog in the rectory, so he kept palming him off on students—six times he was returned, once on the same day. Finally a boy from a farm took him to keep. That is, as we learned later, until Yank was shot by a neighboring farmer for killing sheep.

Yank II was a dachshund who came into my life after I moved to Chicago. Joel Wells who, as you will see, never took kindly to my pets, once described him as "an overfed, overbred dachshund who will eliminate on no other paper than the *New York Times* and who wouldn't retrieve a stick if it were coated with *pate de foie gras.*"

Despite Mr. Wells, I maintain that Yank II was a lovable dog, although I will admit he was a bit neurotic. (I certainly do not believe the oft-heard calumny that a neurotic dog results from a neurotic master, rather I blame his neurosis on his former mistress who, for reasons never disclosed, had named him "Daisy Mae.") Yank suffered from claustrophobia. A closed room with Yank inside was quickly filled with anguished howls and if this outcry did not bring immediate release, he would roll on the floor and feign complete collapse. He was sensitive in other ways, too: if he detected a harsh note in your voice or if a visitor did not show what he considered a proper display of affection, he would sit on the floor with his back to the offender for an hour or two—the length of time depending on the extent of the slight. He was also rather insistent about getting his own way. Unfortunately, he discovered that one method of showing his displeasure if his wishes were not my command was to disgorge the contents of his stomach in the middle of the living room. Seemingly, he could do this at will and found it most effective in dealing wtih me. Nothing was effective, however, when he tried to chase the janitor's German shepherd out of the yard—he came through the battle much scarred but otherwise unfazed.

Yank II was a dog with very definite convictions. He ate only one meal a day, but if his dinner was not ready at 4:00 P.M. or if, even more shocking, his meal had not been garnished with chicken livers, he would stalk from the kitchen and could not be persuaded to eat until hours later—unless he thought he could sneak his food without my noticing. I presume the reason for his uncompromising attitude was his frequent trouble with hiccups and with nightmares, requiring him to watch his diet.

Our biggest dispute came during a record-breaking cold wave when around 3:00 A.M. he awakened me and managed to convey the idea that he wanted to test the night air for himself. I grumbled but stood patiently for fifteen minutes on the back porch with the snow falling on my gray locks and the wind whipping around my bony knees. Back to bed and asleep for only an hour when Yank II again decided he needed my guide services. I muttered "To hell with you, Bub," or words to that effect and went back to sleep, only to learn, when a peculiar sensation aroused me from slumber, that Yank had chosen my bed as the beneficiary of what he had intended for the cold, cold ground.

Eventually Yank II flew off to dog heaven and Yank III, another dachshund, took over. It pains me to write about her since she was the victim of one of the more shameful episodes in my life. A few months after she arrived Yank developed a state of deep melancholia whenever I left for work, a condition she proclaimed by moaning and barking. A spiteful neighbor whom Yank routinely snubbed complained to the apartment manager. I was warned that something must be done. To my everlasting disgrace I did it: I took poor Yank to a veterinarian who debarked her. The noise problem seemed to be solved, except that my conscience would hurt me every time the poor dog tried to bark and no sound came through. It was particularly sad when she was inadvertently locked in a closet for several hours and could not make me aware of her imprisonment. But, to my surprise and to Yank's delight, her vocal chords mended and I decided that it was time for Yank to become a suburbanite. My good friend John Drahos had been subverting my relationship with the dog for many months by bringing meat to her whenever he came to visit and surreptitiously feeding her when my back was turned. He joyfully adopted Yank III and that ended my dog days.

I had no intention of becoming a cat owner—a ridiculous expression since no one ever "owns" a cat. The late vocation was thrust upon me. As I mentioned earlier, the Thomas More Association suffered a sharp depression in the 80s and we were forced to move from the loop to a run-down building in a less desirable area —but an area which has since become Chicago's Soho. Here we faced a new menace: rats and mice. Not only did they leave reminders of their presence on many of the desks at night but they would often race through the office in the daytime, neither of which practice endeared them to the staff who eventually delivered a rather unfriendly ultimatum. We tried various solutions including a professional exterminator but the rodents were too long in the service to be foiled by scientific methods. Finally, in desperation we obtained Maggie from the city pound, only hours before her scheduled execution. In two nights she had the rats and mice on the run and was forced to lavish her attention on giant cockroaches which she would turn on their back and play kickball with.

Maggie could not be called a lovable or endearing cat. She had obviously been raised in an alley and she mistrusts all humans—even attempts to pet her are met with an angry swipe. In *The Critic,* Joel Wells described her as "a female of unknown provenance, steely gaze and razor claws." He seemed to resent the fact that Maggie would leave the victims of her night's kill in only one place, the doorway to my office. "How did she know that he was one who would decide her future," he asked. Furthermore, he claims, "Our CEO (that's me) praised her prowess far and wide; he let her oversee the intricacies of the business day from his windowsill; he, who was wont to dismember errant suppliers and tardy employees with his tongue, began to talk silly baby cat talk to her. When certain playful underlings sought to make sport of Maggie and run wind-up mice across the floor, he issued a memo against the mistreatment and harassment of cats in general and Maggie in particular which would serve as a worthy addition to the Bill of Rights."

Joel's biggest gripe, however, was that Maggie showed her dislike of him from the very first day she arrived at our offices. He explains, "I would watch her out of the corner of my eye and, even when she was apparently sound asleep on a radiator, she would sense this and open her own baleful eye and regard me with naked malevolence. From some fifteen available office chairs, she singled out mine to sleep on during the height of her shedding season; no matter how often I cleaned it or how ingeniously I covered it with sharp objects like staples and letter openers, I would return the next morning to find the defenses scattered on the floor and the chair covered with a new fur coat.

"All this is easily chalked up to coincidence and my personal prejudice against cats, you may protest. True, but what about this: I stayed late several evenings to work on this very article. One evening I left one page of the manuscript in the typewriter and the rest stacked beside it. The next morning the page in the machine had been mutilated by shredding and a bottle of rubber cement had been tipped onto the balance of the papers."

So much for Joel Wells' paranoia and on to the saga of Maggie and me. There was very little heat in our dingy offices during the week and absolutely none on weekends so I decided to carry Maggie home Friday nights and return her Monday morning during the winter months. Maggie adjusted well to her new home—too well. When Monday mornings came she would hide under the bed and fight vigorously any attempt to place her in the cat carrier, unlike her Friday night conduct when she would jump into the container. I finally gave in and Maggie became a full-time member of my household.

Unfortunately, Maggie and I immediately clashed: I had read that it was very easy to teach a cat to use the human toilet and in the interest of efficiency I proceeded to initiate her training. Contrary to what the experts maintained, Maggie was not about to change her toilet habits. I scrupulously followed instructions but Maggie not only refused to cooperate—she proceeded to have all of her eliminations on the carpet in various rooms of my apartment. Obviously, I gave in to her unwillingness to change and (unless she wants to punish me for some imagined slight) she now uses a litter box.

Later, whether the reason was inability to adjust to retirement or something even more deep-seated, Maggie became a feline version of a contemplative and obviously drastic action was called for. A kind and good friend of mine who loves and understands cats and who presides over six of them suggested a solution: Maggie needed a companion and she would furnish same—a young, energetic playful orange tabby. In the best tradition of Tennessee Williams, I named the new boarder "Big Daddy." (And when Big Daddy started to push Maggie around, Abbie Jane Wells, my mother-confessor from Juneau, Alaska, wrote me: "What did you expect when you saddled him with that name—of course, he would push a female around.")

Maggie and Big Daddy and I have had many adventures since then, but I have been told that next to stories about children cat stories rank highest on the boredom scale, so I will spare you, or deprive you, depending on your viewpoint, further fascinating anecdotes.

But I cannot end this treatise on pets without at least a brief mention of my latest enthusiasm—pigeons.

Until I became interested in pigeons I did not realize the extent or the depths of the prejudice against these beautiful birds. Pigeon-lovers, in which category I am now proud to be counted, are the loneliest of minorities and, as with pigeons themselves, are continually subjected to persecution.

My fondness for pigeons came about because our office is on the sixth floor and there is a fire escape outside my windows. One snowy day a sparrow made it up that high and it occurred to me that he and his friends might be hard put to find food. Providing bird seed was no problem and the sparrows flocked in. So did pigeons.

We no longer have sparrows, but we do have ten pigeons who depend on me for their daily bread, except for weekends, of course. When I arrive each morning the scout pigeon (who has been assigned to herald my presence) alerts the crew and they all fly in for breakfast. It'a heartwarming sight, at least for me. But, as with everything in life, there are drawbacks. One of the pigeons, whom I have named "Jackie," is picked on by the others, probably because he is smaller than the rest, and I don't seem to be able to protect him. A further problem is that my colleagues predict we will be evicted on that inevitable day when the wife of the building owner walks below our window and is the recipient of pigeon largesse, if I might so describe it. Until that day, however, I find pigeon-watching a most satisfying way of life. I recommend it.

12) Label Me Eclectic

WE go by various names—"cafeteria Catholics," "cultural Catholics," "pick and choose Catholics," or (my favorite) "eclectic Catholics." And we are not much admired by anybody, including ourselves. The right-wing sees us as heretics; liberals find us far too traditional. As frequently happens with middle-of-the-roaders we are vulnerable to attack from both lanes.

After twenty years pundits are still discussing the pronouncements of the Second Vatican Council. Despite mutterings from conservatives, most experts hail it for bringing the Church into the 20th century. And rightly so. The Council was a triumph, surprising as it was exciting. But the cost has been high, particularly among Catholics over forty.

When I was growing up we Catholics were secure, even smug, in our faith. We knew we had all the answers; we knew that the other churches—sects was the preferred word—taught totally false doctrines and their members were deluded. (They might be saved, of course, if they were "invincibly" ignorant.) We knew our Church had never changed and never would change; we knew why the mass would always be in Latin (surely the vernacular would degrade the Sacred Mysteries); we knew how to use sun-time to postpone the eating-before-communion deadline another hour; we knew that the pope should be an Italian because Italians could rise above nationalism better than any other group. We knew that Martin Luther was a dirty old man who suffered from constipation and indulged in foul language; we knew that no good Catholic would join the YMCA or contribute to the Salvation Army Doughnut Drive; we knew that the chief reason Henry VIII defected and founded his own church was that he was oversexed; we knew that priests were men apart, men of great spiritual and intellectual attainment, made supermen by grace of office; we knew that criticizing or arguing with a priest could be sinful and certainly brought bad luck.

Some of us learned about occult compensation and the principle of double-effect: under what conditions you could go through a red traffic light at three in the morning, how to justify gypping the phone company or any other public utility, and what made fudging your income tax less sinful than other kinds of fraud. All of us knew that every sin connected with sex was mortal and we suspected that anything you took pleasure in probably led to sin. We knew that eating meat on Friday or missing mass on Sundays and Holy Days of Obligation would condemn our souls to eternal hellfire. We knew that everything the pope said, whether or not it was *per se* infallible—Latin phrases were popular in the old Church—had better be believed without question; we explained away the bad popes by arguing that, if true, this was simply additional proof that the Church was protected by the Holy Spirit. As Catholics we bought the whole package. There was only one kind of Catholic in those days; you accepted it all and achieved salvation or you took none if it and your soul was lost forever and ever.

No Catholic that I knew, even those whose faith had so deteriorated that they were willing to mumble privately about the hierarchy, ever expected changes in our unchanging Church, the Church we had known since childhood. And news of the election of "tired, old" Pope John XXIII only confirmed our belief. Before long, however, we came to learn that the Pope was not just another superannuated Italian curialist but rather a man unique, whose brief reign as pope would deeply and irrevocably alter the lives of almost every Catholic. When the Council was announced, most of us were vague about what a council was or what it could do and we expected little from it except reaffirmation of the status quo. Eventually there were rumors about possible radical reforms, but no one put much credence in them. And even when the Council had ended, its potential impact was not generally realized.

Almost imperceptibly, before most of us knew what was happening, the Church changed and in some manner almost every Catholic changed, consciously or unconsciously, willingly or not. In the words of Anna Quindlen, "The sovereignty of the church over the lives of its citizens was beginning, very slowly, to crumble." Reform was in swing, not in full swing at first but in sufficient force to please the moderates. Then pressures which we did not realize had been building for a long, long time finally blew. Inevitably into operation went the law of rising expectations—once extremist Catholics saw that change was possible, no crusade was considered too woolly or too revolutionary. We witnessed the appalling spectacle of those who would not move with the changing church and of those heedless and headless liberals who insisted on running like hell in any and sometimes every direction—not for them deliberate speed. In some ways reform became a rout, calling to mind my father's malediction: "It's enough to physic a rat."

In the midst of this turmoil came the papal encyclical *Humanae Vitae* and to almost everyone whose thinking was to the left of Cardinal Ottaviani—our chief whipping boy in those days—confusion and bitterness ensued. To be followed by internecine warfare that has continued to this day and shows no signs of abating. (One commentator, Protestant theologian John MacQuarrie of Union Theological Seminary, questioned: "One sometimes wonders whether the Roman Catholic Church is in process of renewal or whether we are witnessing its dissolution.") Positions hardened and fanatics grabbed for the headlines. The liberal extremists captured the media, winning both extensive coverage and sympathetic treatment, but the right wing had the most influence with the Vatican and, as a result of intense letter-writing campaigns, downed several of its targets, notably a widely-used catechism. The outflow of priests and nuns became a deluge: commitments and vows forgotten or ignored in the rush—some into the arms of loved ones; others into the limbo of obscurity; and still others trying to have it both ways, to enjoy their new freedom but demanding to be treated as clerical experts on Mother Church.

If this world were efficiently run, the turmoil in the Church would have quieted after these many years and the extremists would have found some other outlet for their frustrations. Nothing like that has happened. At best, we have learned to live with, or within, a Church that is too often characterized by dissension, by unrest, by apathy. Today's Catholics are a people of lowered expectations—most of us would settle for some sort of stability based on compromises between the Church of the past and modern world.

I suggest that every American Catholic is an eclectic Catholic, although most may not admit it. Even the rigid traditionalists are not so "obedient" as to accept the new Mass. You can readily spot them: they ignore the now established handshake at the Sign of Peace; although Pope John Paul II is a favorite of the Right, American bishops, individually and collectively, are their frequent targets, but, of course, they do not consider their criticism anticlerical. At the opposite pole, the social activists, like too many other extremist Catholics, are convinced they alone have the truth—about Nicaragua, El Salvador, nuclear war, or any other subject they have taken a stand on. I find religious fanatics, Right, Left and Muddled, irritating, snobbish and obstinate in their beliefs. As would be proved to any reasonably-minded reader inflicted with a few issues of *National Catholic Reporter* and *The Wanderer*—and despite my close association with the *Reporter,* as a Director and Chairman of the Board during its earliest and most glorious (Robert Hoyt) days—I must admit *The Wanderer,* though mostly comic, is far the more interesting of the two.

It should be obvious to even the most casual observer that the stereotype Catholic no longer exists in America. Instead, there are millions of American Catholics who differ in their concept of Catholicism, perhaps only slightly but nevertheless they do differ. As Barbara Grizutti Harrison wrote in *The New York Times,* "It is increasingly hard for a Catholic of any nationality to find his or her 'place' in a fragmented church, one that sometimes seems more like a candy store than a monolith."

All of which is prelude to my own apologia, without which—so I am told—any backward look (such as these chapters) would be incomplete. Like the rest of American Catholics, I ain't what I used to be. Not that I would maintain my present faith is an improved model, or that I am a better or happier Catholic. But I do suggest that I am less neurotic, more open-minded (though some might disagree), less encumbered with legalisms, less prejudiced. Missing from my life—and not without some qualms—are confession, fasting and other lenten observances, abstinence of meat on Fridays, acquiring of indulgences, awe of priests, the rosary, rigid adherence to such beliefs as infallibility, negative sexual morality, the existence of limbo, purgatory and hell, and other practices and doctrines once a seemingly integral part of me.

Not that all my problems have been solved. The present state of the liturgy is a continuing irritation. I agree with Alec Guiness who deplores "the banality and vulgarity of the translation" and describes the general tones as "rather like a BBC radio broadcast for tiny tots." I would even settle for the return of the Latin mass. I find the present rigid position on ordination of women incomprehensible and impractical; the exalted role of "experts" in religious education, "ministry," liturgy and whatever other area they can encroach upon a pain in the ass; and the rise of the laity a portent of dismal days ahead, what with chancery office toadies, frustrated actors and actresses preening themselves in the pulpit and similar supernumeraries. Although we have managed to ditch a good deal of the legalisms, none of which should play any part in religion, there are still too many and small hope they will be disappearing. I am opposed to married priests for many reasons, not the least of which is that defected priests who opted out and married with or without permission now whiningly demand to have it both ways. The Church is well shorn of most of them. Just as it could well do without many of the "liberal" publicity seekers (some of the worst being nuns) who issue declarations, sign manifestos and otherwise make damn fools of themselves. And yes, I am opposed to abortion. (It is unfortunate that the Vatican has loused up the abortion controversy by its intractable attitude toward birth control, masturbation and other sexual peccadilloes that demand a new approach for the 21st century.)

But with all that said, I must emphasize that for me there is no appealing or convincing alternative to Catholicism.

13) To Bury The Dead

IF you're like me, your every nerve tingles at the mere mention of an Irish wake. All my life I have yearned to be a mourner at one of those rollicking affairs.

Being Irish and being a fairly regular frequenter of funeral ceremonials, I once thought that someday I, too, could boast of participating in the real thing. But I was born too late. By the time I had reached the waking age, all the Irish I knew had begun to seek respectability by aping the stuffier attitudes and mores of their conservative neighbors. The traditional Irish approach to death was a twentieth-century victim to Irish-American conformity. Not only the Irish wake but the Irish spirit of looking at the bright, or possibly the comic, side of death gave way to Puritan grimness and unrelieved sorrow and solemnity. Gone forever are the days of tilting the casket against the wall, placing a twenty-five cent cigar in the mouth of the corpse and drinking good health to all present.

I'll admit that this sort of shenanigan may seem the weest bit disrespectful to the more squeamish, but I suggest that is is much closer to the ideal than the pagan rituals, full of despair and self-pity, we are accustomed to.

Not only was I cheated out of enjoying an Irish wake, but I learned fairly early in life, "Don't try to be funny at a funeral." The first glimmering of this profound truth came to me when my father died.

Try as hard as he could, and he did try, believe me, my father never quite succeeded in being on time for Mass. Day after day, and Sunday after Sunday, at some

121

point before the Gospel the squeaking door of the church announced my father's arrival. So accustomed was the congregation to this ritual that no one, except possibly a visitor, ever looked up. No matter how much advance preparation he made the night before, no matter how early he would arise, the result was always the same.

The morning of my father's funeral it occurred to me that this would be the first time he would arrive for Mass at the expected hour. The more I thought of this, the more unseemly it became. Of course, he could hardly be late for the funeral, particuarly since my brother was offering the Mass, but the very least we could do was to delay the whole ceremony fifteen minutes. I knew my father would have appreciated the jest and with a little persuasion I managed to convince my mother and the other members of the family that no other course of action was desirable.

Unforunately, no one—not one single friend, relative, acquaintance or bystander—was amused. As for the pastor, who, unbeknown to me, had been conducting a vigorous campaign to commence weddings and funerals at the precise, announced moment—his wrath was sufficient to give birth to six medium-size or two extra-large ulcers. Although I would be the first to admit that this was no belly-shaking idea, I still insist that under the circumstances it was not too bad, and I deplore the fact that my family and I were alone in appreciating it.

I wasn't able to do much in the way of enlivening my father's wake and I really didn't try. In this case, we were not concerned so much with reviving the tradition of the Irish wake as in preventing what by this time was a characteristic of all Herr wakes—the family jangle.

My father's family was large and well scattered. Members came together solely for the purpose of burying one of the clan. As in all normal families, there were differences of opinion, but in our family these differences could be aired only in the presence of a corpse. When the tribe was formally summoned for the last rites of one of its fellows, old feuds were dug up and dusted off, tempers were triggered and everyone looked forward to a good emotional catharsis.

I well remember the time that some busybody strayed from the scene of action during the burial of an uncle and discovered, by comparing gravestones, that my grandfather was much younger than my grandmother. For some reason this shocking fact had been kept well hidden and the revelation, set off during a pause in the post-funeral feasting, resulted in a tizzy beating anything I had heard before or since.

Another time, a relative who through the years had developed a certain coolness toward the newly deceased, forgave all when the bad news came and set out for the scene of the obsequies. Before going he asked his local florist to order by telegraph a suitable floral remembrance but, since he would be present when the flowers arrived, to omit the sympathy card. He was present, all right, but not for long. The flowers arrived with an unusually large card, inscribed, "Omit sympathy." He didn't even get a chance to explain, which was probably just as well, since no one would have believed his preposterous story.

Most vivid in my memory was the wake for my Uncle Billy. Life had not been kind to Uncle Billy—he was an early victim of automation. In his youth Uncle Billy had but one ambition, to drive the magnificent horse-drawn hearse of the leading undertaker of the town. In one way he was more fortunate than most of us because he achieved this ambition early in life and, except for one brief period when he was suspended for imbibing too much and racing the hearse complete with corpse all over town, he was a man who found fulfillment in his work. Then came the motorized hearse and Uncle Billy, never a man to accept progress, was finished.

For the rest of his life he sat back and contemplated the march of mankind toward destruction. In winter, his chief occupation was a careful scrutiny of all local obituaries with particular emphasis on which undertaker "got him." He was still loyal to his old employers, even though he felt he had been badly used, and if they "got" more than their competitors, he was in a radiant mood for the remainder of the day. He forewent this activity during the summer—for one thing, fewer peole died during the hot months, he maintained, and for another his passion for baseball was all-consuming. He compromised with the machine age to the extent of listening to ball game radio broadcasts, but he refused to learn how to operate the gadget. As a result, "the Mrs.," as he called his wife Mary, was never able to go visiting except in the morning or on days when no game was scheduled. But she loved Uncle Billy as much in his declining years as when he had been a dashing hero with his coal-black horses, and never once did she complain.

Uncle Billy's wake was proceeding with unaccustomed smoothness when one of my uncles, who unfortunately was inclined to be flip, gazed at the remains and mumbled quietly, or so he thought, "Well, at least he won't have to snag stogie butts any more." There's probably no need to tell you that this reference to Uncle Billy's favorite outdoor sport was ill-timed to resound at the very moment when all the various groups of mourners had paused for breath, and even those who claimed to be hard of hearing missed not a word. In all charity, I will draw the mantle of silence over the ensuing rumble.

My favorite funeral scene, however, was one that I did not witness personally, but heard about from my father who was present. The corpse this time was the town reprobate, something of an alcoholic prodigy. According to all reports, he had not committed one good deed since he reached the age of reason. Alcohol seemed to agree with him and he lived, if you will pardon the expression, to a ripe old age.

His two maiden sisters, his only relatives, were everything that he was not. Respected pillars of the Church they were—so respectable that the more cynical wondered if they might not have been the cause of their brother's downfall.

When their brother died, they determined that he must be buried from the Church, no matter the obstacles, and there were plenty. When they first approached their old Irish pastor, he was horrified at the suggestion. But copious tears and explicit references to two lifetimes devoted to the service of the parish as well as the possibility of a large bequest someday could not be ignored. The pastor grudgingly compromised on an afternoon funeral with the barest minimum of ceremony.

No sooner had he made the compromising promise and the grateful "girls" had left the rectory, than he regretted his magnanimity. To the very moment of the funeral, he fumed and fretted and riled up his stomach juices, but, of course, he couldn't go back on his word.

Dressed in full cope, accompanied by altar boys, he

solemnly approached the casket. Then something snapped! He pounded the casket vigorously and yelled, "Twice in Church, and both times they had to carry him in." All passion spent, he proceeded to calmly intone the prayers for the dead in Latin.

As a result of unburdening myself in conversation and in print on wakes that were part of our family lore, I have been privileged to be the recipient of many stories about wakes and funerals from friends. It has been satisfying to learn that I am not alone in enjoying, if that is the right word, the unexpected developments that some-times accompany the better kind of funerary rituals. The Church in Ireland, so I am told, has managed to outlaw the traditional Irish wake on the auld sod and, as previously observed, snooty young Irish-Americans seem to be too good for that sort of thing. Other ethnic groups are following suit and WASP wakes have never been the occasion of much hilarity. The problem, as I see it, is that death has become institutionalized and must therefore be treated solemnly and perfunctorily. There is room no longer for humor and even very little consideration for grief—let's be fast and efficient and then on about our business. For the sake of future historians who might otherwise have no way of knowing what wakes and funerals were like before they became soulless, I add these notes about the good old days.

A few years ago, in a small Ohio town the father of a friend of mine died a particularly tragic death, leaving an inconsolable widow. But even she found that life is not all tears when an aged, and we must presume slightly confused, neighbor marched in the night of the wake, enthusiastically shook the widow's hand and announced: "Congratulations, Mrs. Michaels."

Which story reminds me that most humor at wakes is unintentional. Another friend, after consoling a widow with three young children, decided she should also offer sympathy to the children. However, being single and out of touch with the younger generation, she was uncertain how to approach them. After a few tongue-tied moments, she found herself asking, "And how was your weekend, children?" For some reason the children did not answer her.

On the other hand, you can't excuse some wake bloopers on the grounds they were unintentional. Perhaps the worst example of the kind of remark which even the Holy Spirit could not see fit to forgive occurred, I am told, in Springfield, Illinois. A young child had died unexpectedly and the parents were grieving. Just ahead of my friends in the sympathy line were a middle-aged couple who exclaimed to the saddened parents: "We know just how you feel—our little dog died last month and we have been mourning ever since."

The easiest possible way to fall from grace at a wake, I suggest, is by too quickly reacting to the usual statement from the bereaved, "Thank you for coming." Many are the unwary who, caught unprepared, lapse into "I was delighted to come." Even worse, was the retort of a Chicago friend who said, obviously without thinking, "Thank you for inviting me."

One of the best stories that came my way was told by a priest and it's too good not to retell even if it belongs in the prewake category. It happened some years ago on a snowy night when the priest was called out to give the "last rites," as we then knew them, to the wife of a farmer. The farmhouse was on top of a hill and the struggle to reach it with the howling wind and the driving snow required all the energy he had. But climb it he did, only to find that the woman had been long dead and that the hearse was on the way. The undertaker arrived soon and with the help of an assistant transferred the behemoth of a corpse—about 280 pounds of dead weight, they estimated—from the bed to a stretcher and departed. A few minutes later, while the priest was still consoling the family, the undertaker returned and asked Father if he would please step outside. Once on the porch, he said: "Keep those people busy as long as you can don't let them come out here. The corpse rolled off the damn stretcher, down the hill and is lost in some lousy snowbank. God knows when we will find her."

To the same priest I am indebted for the story of the funeral of a father who died leaving, as we say, six strapping sons. They loved the old man dearly, so dearly that their grief on the morning of the funeral seemed to demand at least a few drinks to help them bear up. As to be expected, there were more than a few drinks. Appropriately, the boys acted as their father's pallbearers and when it was time to place the casket in the grave—in those barbaric days a casket was not left in a chapel but was actually buried in full view of the mourners—they finished their father's obsequies in style. "One, two, three, in with him," cried the oldest brother. And in he went. Fortunately, the casket was of good quality and withstood the shock.

I recall that at my older brother's wake the children of a distant relative sat in the back of the funeral parlor while one of the girls read them ghost stories—which I considered an odd literary choice considering the circumstances. And this brings up the problem of taking children to wakes, a problem that sharply divided a husband and wife I know. The husband won out, as husbands sometimes do, and the children attended the wake. As they were kneeling in front of the coffin, the youngest piped up: "Daddy, why have they glued grandpa's collar to his neck?" As the mother rushed the children out of the room, the father looked more closely at the corpse: sure enough, the collar had been glued, but obviously not well.

Now if the harvest is over
And the world cold
Give me the bonus of laughter
As I lose hold.

John Betjman

An Afterword

IT'S a brave man who permits himself to be bookended by Joel Wells and the present clerical trouble maker. I do not, however, propose in this afterword to imitate Mr. Herr's (some folks call him "Dan", his friends call him "Mr. Herr"—a custom that originated, I believe, when he protested about the priests who called him "Dan" but insisted that he call them "Father." Ah, those were the days!) courage and try to match wits with Joel Wells.

I must pause, however, before turning to the serious purposes of this afterword to note that while Mr. Herr is rarely in error and never in doubt, he is sometimes wrong. In this book, he is wrong about the Latin mass. The reason the English liturgy is so bad is that we priests had become such sloppy liturgists in Latin. Take yourself to an Anglican church if you want to see what taste and dignity can do for English as a language of worship. (Don't go there, however, if you want to find people.) It will require a generation to exorcise from Catholicism the ill effects of clerical mumbling and bumbling in the so-called "mystical" and "reverent" and "mysterious" Latin mass. The only mystery is why so many lay people didn't realize how slovenly we liturgists were.

In real life Mr. Herr's errors normally have to do with movies (too frequently wrong) restaurants (more often wrong than you would think) mystery stories (practically never wrong) and Chicago politics (practically always wrong).

Otherwise his charism of infallibility is positively papal.

I transmit his affection for furry creatures which so bemuses Mr. Wells (you can call him "Joel") in great part because I share it. I would not, however, maintain an Irish wolfhound—my favorite among the furry ones—in my house in the absence of children to keep it amused.

To become properly serious as a practicing academic must, I propose two paradigms to convert Dan Herr, kicking and screaming, into a symbol: the transition paradigm and the dissonance reducing paradigm. The two, I contend, complement one another and illuminate the present condition of American Catholicism rather neatly.

Catholics have been caught for the last quarter-century and are likely to be caught for the next quarter-century in the intersection of two transitions, from immigrant to suburban professional and from Counter Reformation to ecumenical age. At one level this book can be read as an illustration of that process and of the kind of adjustment to it that American Catholics have made: a certain amount of nostalgic regret for what has been left behind, but no serious desire to return to it; a powerful loyalty to the tradition and an inability to accept seriously the posturings and pronouncements of those who claim to be its authoritative interpreters. In this paradigm, Dan Herr is Catholic Everyman. The remarkable fact is not that we have undergone these transitions—in retrospect they both were inevitable—but that we have survived them as well as we have. Most American Catholics (roughly nine out of ten) have elected to follow the same paths that Dan Herr has followed, if not with quite so much pungent commentary on the present incumbents of the seats of Moses and Aaron.

Dissonance reduction—the elimination of as much intellectual and emotional conflict as possible—has not been difficult for most Catholic laity. They like the new church and are willing to give up what was lost. They are untroubled by the insensitivities of their leadership because they don't have to listen to them.

It is considerably more difficult to reduce dissonance if your daily work is church related. Not to put too fine an edge on things, you have to live with the idiots every day. (Incidentally, Mr. Herr skirts gracefully in this book any speculation on the enormously successful career he could have had in the world of secular journalism, if he had not chosen the vocation he did.) Moreover, you see others all around you running for cover because they can't take the heat. The temptation is to get out yourself, to protect yourself from being the last priest to jump ship after everyone else has left, to quit, to move to the margins and reduce your dissonance by playing the role of the professional "ex"—ex-priest, ex-Catholic, ex-editor of an ex-publication.

(I do not suggest that all resigned priests behave this way. On the contrary, like Hugh Donlon in one of my stories, most do not. I do suggest, with Mr. Herr, that those who do play the role—I could provide names on request—are by now an almost intolerable pain in sensitive parts of the anatomy.)

It's one way to adjust if you are at the center of the institution and the noise becomes intolerable.

Dan Herr chose a far more constructive method of dissonance reduction—you stay and fight. Many Catholic publishing ventures, often with the subsidizing resources of a religious order behind them, chose to fold when their readers suddenly (almost over night) found other attractions on which to spend their money. Since then they have been on the margins, one way or another, playing a role which is a mix of Cassandra and Jeremiah, and blaming everyone but themselves.

The Thomas More Association chose to fight back. While one can never be certain of permanency in the volatile Catholic marketplace these days, the fight back has kept the wolf and other demons away from the door, which is no small achievement. And the resurgence of *The Critic*—in what I at any rate find a much more attractive guise—reminds me of the line from *Ballad of the White Horse,* quoted by the Times (of London) at the North African landings in 1942: "It is the high time, King Alfred cried, The high tide and the turn."

He and his colleagues did not quit. They stayed and they fought back. The quitters may not think that admirable. I do. The Thomas More response is a paradigm for Catholic survival that is worthy of respect, admiration and imitation.

Don't let *them* get you.

Mr. Herr would accuse me of sentimentality if I said the battle of The Thomas More Association for survival and to reach "the turn" was gallant. So I will be content with saying that, like his rebound from serious heart surgery, the battle was graceful.

And, damn it, graceful response to crisis is a rarity in the Catholic Church these days, a veritable treasure hidden in a field.

If there is any digging going on, then, it is digging for buried treasure.

Andrew M. Greeley